JESUS–
HUMAN
and
DIVINE

To know Jesus who is called Christ in the knowledge of faith is itself a requirement of faith. And the New Testament is not vague regarding Him. The Biblical Christ is in a valid sense the historical Jesus; and the historical Jesus is the living and reigning Lord. It is in this assurance that the present slender volume has been written: more particularly it has been written as a help to the general Christian student to come to a firmer understanding of the Saviour in whom his faith is reposed and his hope is centred. That is not of authentic Christian faith which refuses the affirmation that Jesus Christ has come in flesh; nor yet which withholds the personal confession of Him as, 'My Lord and my God'. The following pages seek to confirm for those who believe, that He is rightly acknowledged as both Human and Divine. And to challenge those who may read, not of faith, to face squarely the question of the ages, Who then is this Jesus which is called Christ?

JESUS–
HUMAN
and
DIVINE

H. D. McDONALD
Ph.D.(Lond.), D.D.(Lond.)

**ZONDERVAN
PUBLISHING HOUSE**
OF THE ZONDERVAN CORPORATION
GRAND RAPIDS, MICHIGAN 49506

Copyright © 1968   H. D. McDonald

Second printing (Zondervan CEP series) 1970
Third printing 1973
Fourth printing 1974

SBN 7208 0022 6

Printed in the United States of America

Contents

THE REDEEMING REALITY
How sayest thou that the Son of Man
must be lifted up?

THE EXALTED REALITY
Ought not Christ to have suffered and to
have entered into His glory?

THE ULTIMACY OF JESUS CHRIST
THE ALPHA AND OMEGA

INTRODUCTION

The following pages should be regarded as introductory to the study of New Testament Christology. What was asked of the writer was to produce some fairly easy work which would help the general Christian student to set off on a more sure understanding of the Saviour in whom his faith is reposed and his hope centred. To this programme we have endeavoured to remain faithful. We have, therefore, set out with the presupposition that the data of the New Testament are to be taken on their face value; with the conviction, that is, that the Synoptic Gospels assure to faith its historical basis and the Fourth Gospel authenticates for faith its spiritual valuation and the rest of the New Testament demonstrates for faith Christ's relation to the fellowship of the Church and the needs of the world.

We have not, consequently, entered upon a discussion of the relation between the 'Jesus of History' and 'The Christ of Faith'; nor have we sought to isolate a 'Heilgeschichte' Christ or a 'Kerygmatic' Christ from the Gospels' presentation of Him. There is here no new quest for the historical Jesus since for us the Jesus of the New Testament is the only Christ we can know; and it is this Christ who is focal and final in the Christian gospel. We have not, then, taken sides with Barth against Harnack, or with Pannenberg against Bultmann. This is not because we regard the issues they have raised as unimportant. It is rather because the Christ to be known is the Christ of the whole New Testament.

Put more simply we are seeking to fulfil a more modest purpose, namely this, to give a suggestive presentation of Jesus as Human and Divine. We are not, however, without the hope that the Christian preacher and teacher will find scheme and scope here for their tasks. Ideas may be found in the outline and treatment of the subject

7

which may be filled out for the blessing and benefit of those to be instructed in the truth as it is in Christ Jesus. In this sense what follows may be taken in the style of a 'Dogmatic', in the sense, that is, that Heinrick Ott says, 'Dogmatics is preaching to preachers'.

Rudolf Bultmann has stated that, 'The interpretation of the biblical writings is not subject to conditions different from those applying to all other kinds of literature'. This is true and false. It is true because we are dealing with a literature; with what is written. But it is false if we regard the New Testament as like, in every respect, all other kinds of literature. This it is not. For the truth of the matter is, that the New Testament with the Old, as the closing paragraph of the Preface of the Revised Standard Version of the Scriptures says, 'is more than a historical document to be preserved. And it is more than a classic of English literature to be cherished and admired. It is a record of God's dealing with men, of God's revelation of Himself and His will. It records the deeds and life of Him in whom the Word of God became flesh and dwelt among men. The bible carries its full message, not to those who regard it simply as a heritage of the past and praise its literary style, but to those who read it and discern and understand God's Word to men'.

I would like to take the opportunity of thanking Professor Richard N. Longeneker of the Trinity Evangelical Divinity School, Deerfield, Illinois, U.S.A., whose own field of study is that of New Testament History and Theology to which he has made important contributions, for being kind enough to read through and correct the 'proofs'. It was an imposition passing on a work so meagre to him, but he very graciously accepted this added burden and has put me in his debt. It was a delight to spend a Semester at Trinity as Visiting-Professor and the experience has been to me most enriching. The arrival of the 'proofs' at that time gave me the opportunity of calling on Professor Longenecker for help. Whatever blemishes in style, content and the like remain are all of my doing and for them I am alone responsible. In spite, however, of these it is hoped that what follows will be useful to those who seek an answer to the question, Who is this Jesus that is called Christ?

'The Christian God is also a carpenter's Son from Nazareth. "Foxes have holes, and the birds of the air have nests, but the Son of Man hath not where to lay His head." And yet Christ appears in the Christian designation as one with the Creator of the world and the Ruler of the world. Out of debasement, He suddenly is exalted. The change appears strange, yet so natural.'

ALEX HÄGERSTRÖM

'It is by no means true that we must blind ourselves in order to be able to believe. On the contrary, we must so understand that faith goes along with the greatest clearheadedness ever revealed to us men—the clearheadedness and realism of the men of the Bible . . . We have the promise that as Christians we shall be clearsighted men who are permitted to know the secrets of God.'

HELMUT THEILICKE

THE HUMAN REALITY
What manner of Man is this?

Chapter One

THE FACT OF HIS REAL HUMANITY

THE EVIDENCE OF HIS HUMAN LIFE

It was in the calm which followed the storm which Jesus had subdued with a word that the question of the ages was framed by those astonished disciples of His; What manner of man is this that even the winds and the sea obey Him? (Matt. 8. 27; cf. Mark 4. 41; Luke 8. 25). What manner of man is this? The tone of the question suggests that His disciple band was becoming aware of something unique and unaccountable about the Jesus of Nazareth with whom they had thrown in their lot. He was beginning to impress them with the fact that He was somehow solitary and unique. Just now He had slept on in the midst of a howling storm which had suddenly churned the Lake of Galilee into a treacherous whirlpool, and which had brought the occupants, expert fishermen though they were, nigh to disaster. Yet He was asleep as if indifferent to their concern and their safety; and not apparently in the least bothered about His own. When they wake Him He quietens the raging whirlpool with a word. Immediately they realize that He who appeared indifferent is surely invincible. What manner of man is this?

Yet he had been *sleeping*: this is the important fact. For this makes clear to us that however unique and unaccountable He was, He was no phantom being. However more than man He was, He was not less. He was quite literally and truly a man.

13

It is with this fact about Jesus we must begin: about the evidence for it and the importance of it.

We can look at the evidence for the human reality of the man Jesus from the point of view of the 'outer court' of His natural life and the 'holy place' of His moral and spiritual personality. The 'holy of holies' of his ultimate being is outside our consideration at this point.

There is no doubt that Jesus had a body no less real than that of other men. True, He does not seem to have suffered from illness. There was a certain physical robustness about Him which made it possible for Him to take long journeys on foot and to spend long nights in prayer. This fact distinguishes Him significantly from the founders of other religions. Mohammed, for example, was a sick man and Buddha, at least in his later years, was a weak man. But are sickness and weakness necessary to human existence in its genuine humanness? It is not obvious that they are. Like sin, they mark us all as being less than human; as being fallen humans.

Yet the plain fact is that the man Jesus was truly man; being found in fashion as a man except in those particulars which make man less than man. He came into human life in the human way of natural birth after the lapse of the requisite time (Matt. 1. 25; 2. 1; Luke 2. 7). He had a mother as we all have (Gal. 4. 4). He grew as other boys do, to maturity and manhood (Luke 2. 40). He partook of food (Luke 7. 34-36; 14. 1; 15. 2; 24, 41, 43). He knew what it was to be hungry (Matt. 21. 18; Luke 4. 2) and thirsty (John 19. 28). Robust as we have suggested was His physical frame He did experience fatigue (John 4. 6f.). He was under the necessary limitations of space as are ordinary men and had thus to make His way laboriously from place to place (Luke 8 1; John 4. 4). He felt the indignities and the inhumanities attending a mock trial and a public execution (John 19. 28, 33). While the fact that His death was real and no

temporary loss of consciousness, no swoon, no make-
believe, is attested in the most unconscious and unaffected
manner by one who could not have been conversant
with the essential principles of human anatomy (John
19. 34).

When we pass further into the outer court and closer
to the holy place we are assured that He was still human
in all that here pertains to manhood. He possessed those
human elements of soul which distinguish man from the
animals and which make him more than a different type
of somatic creature. He revealed those properties of
mind, emotion and will, characteristic of the human
individual. He showed His possession of normal mental
processes by asking questions to gain information
(Mark 9. 21; Luke 2. 46-67). Quite clearly He had
studied the Old Testament Scriptures, and learned many
passages by heart, in the village school attached to the
synagogue, as was the custom of the day. The Jewish
elders were particular in this regard; it being provided
that regular instruction for all children should begin at
the age of five or six years. So insisted upon was this requirement that it was regarded as unlawful to live in a
place where there was no school. A city without a school
was deemed worthy of destruction or excommunication.

Not only at His temptations but throughout His
ministry Jesus made abundantly evident that He had
learned well the Bible of His people. But he showed no
less in His discourses, His repartees and His questions
all the signs that His mind worked according to the
normal processes of thinking and reasoning.

At the same time He displayed throughout the
emotions common to all men; the love of family (John
19. 26), of friends (John 15. 15), and even, perhaps, of
country (Matt. 23. 37); as well as the more particular
form of emotive (Mark 10. 21) and the more general
form of complacent love (Mark 14. 8). He could express

the anger of moral indignation, too (Mark 3. 5; 10. 14; Luke 11. 46; John 8. 44). With sorrow He was not unfamiliar (Matt. 26. 37, 38; John 11. 33-36). He knew what it was to 'wail' (klaiō) by reason of disappointment (Luke 19. 41) and to weep (darkuō) by reason of sympathy (John 11. 35). While again and again we read of the compassion which flowed from His noble heart (Matt. 9. 36; 14. 14; 15. 32; 20. 34; Mark 1. 41; 6. 34; 8. 2. etc.).

It seems impossible to doubt, in the light of His own declarations, that Jesus had a will of His own (Matt. 26. 39). It is clear that not only was His will moved by appropriate considerations as is ours (John 7. 1-10), but also that it displayed the same activities and operated by the same forces as are common to all men. Throughout His life in the flesh there were occasions when He had to steel Himself with purpose of will against temptations and to set His face as a flint to the fulfilment of His vocation. What have been called the virtues of the will are particularly exemplified by the steadfastness and persistence with which He continued loyal to His calling despite the contrary suggestions of His friends (Matt. 16. 22) and the consistent hostility of His enemies (Matt. 12. 14; Mark 11. 18).

A true psychological reading of the gospel narratives will, then, secure the one important fact that Jesus possessed those human realities of mind and heart which are fundamental requirements of an actual personality.

But we must press into the inner court, the holy place of His moral and spiritual life. More particularly do we become aware within this vantage-point of what we may refer to as Jesus's religious relation to God. He certainly knew God in an intimate and personal way. It has been rightly remarked that Jesus was not one of the many seekers after God, not even if we call Him one of the successful. He bore witness to God. His understanding of God is a prophetic testimony born out of His inner experience. His knowledge of God was the natural outflow of His intercourse with God. He felt Himself to be in full possession of God; to be in His presence always. He truly knew nothing of the 'nevertheless' of belief; He had never any doubt about God, for God's presence was for Him a living and a felt certainty. He did not regard God as an hypothesis to make the world credible but as the Father who made the world actual.

It was out of this living and felt awareness of God's reality and presence that there sprang His faith, prayer, joy and obedience with reference to God, and His service and patience with reference to man. His trust in God was real and wholehearted. He was not nervous and timid amid life's uncertainties, for to Him everything was in the Father's hands (Matt. 10. 29). It was this burning certainty which accounts for that holy unconcern which characterised His ministry. His strong courage and His serene restfulness of spirit grew out of His absolute confidence and trust in God. There was no restlessness, no flurry, because of the knowledge that He was not labouring without God. He embodied the Old Testament word: He that believeth shall not make haste (Isa. 28. 16; cf. Matt. 11. 28-30).

'Belong to yourself before you belong to others' wrote Bernard of Clairvaux to his pupil, Pope Eugenius II. Jesus went one better than that. He belonged to God first. But He sought to belong to Himself too—in the proper order. It is for this reason He sought the place of solitude before His times of service. He waits that He may be alone. He knows that He needs God, though He shares His life. He is sure of God all the day through and all the way along; but He must talk to Him, must get together with God. Has He not taught us that man needs no spectators, no congregation, no priests when he prays? (Matt. 6. 6). Thus Jesus prays (Mark 1. 35;

6. 46; etc.). His praying was no parade; it meant something. He prayed not simply as an example to His disciples; as a model which they would do well to copy. He prayed because He had need to pray; that He might find refuge under the shadow of the Almighty wings; that He might renew His innermost being in the strength of God and find nerve for the ordeals of living in His reverent trust in His Father.

There is no fear in love. And the love of Jesus for God cast out all fear. Bound up in His love for and trust in God was that joy in God with which all His words and works are permeated. They breathe the spirit of assured joyousness. It was in this attitude of faith, prayer and joy He rendered His full obedience to the will of God. He thus came to accomplish the works of God and having put His hand to the plough He did not look back. Thus was the religious relation of Jesus to God at once both natural and spiritual; the same that is required of all men, but which none but He has met.

When we turn to the manward references of Jesus's religious relation to God we find them all there: candour, compassion, patience and humility, and all else besides which spring out of a man's faith in, communion with and obedience to God. All that it takes to be a man is found in this Man. In this One called Jesus we encounter a human reality.

Coming to the importance of Christ's humanity for faith it must be stressed right away that the Church has always sought to safeguard both its reality and its integrity. In a day when the 'spiritual' was more 'real' than the 'material' it was the actuality of Christ's full human nature which was most in doubt. The apostolic Church had to set its face against the Docetae who questioned the reality of Christ's body and the post-Apostolic Church had to maintain the full integrity of Christ's humanity against the Laodicean bishop,

Apollinarius. The Docetae removed the body of Christ as an illusion and the Apollinarians reduced the humanity of Christ to an incompleteness. Like the Church in Laodicea to which John wrote his special word in the Revelation, the Christ of Apollinarius was neither cold nor hot; neither fully man nor fully God, but a 'glorious mixture' of both. But an illusory Jesus or an incomplete Jesus does not meet the requirements of the gospel. For this reason the First Epistle of John was written to show the necessity of the full humanity of Jesus for faith (1 John 1. 1; 2. 22; 4. 2, 3), and the Epistle to the Hebrews to insist upon the necessity of the full humanness of Jesus for salvation (cf. Heb. 2. 14f).

It is this fundamental gospel fact of the reality and integrity of Christ's humanity which gives reality and integrity to the Incarnation. However the Incarnation is interpreted it is one essential to keep clear in mind that there was no diminution of the human as a result. The Word became *flesh*; and this must be understood in its bald actuality and stark literalness. In the Person of Jesus Christ, He who was eternally with the Father took to Himself a full human life, thereby entering as Son of God into all the conditions of human physical life, as well as into all the conditions of human psychical life. In the man Jesus 'dwelleth all the fulness of the Godhead *bodily*' (Col. 2. 9). It is therefore, as H. R. Mackintosh remarks, the centre of the Catholic faith to see that Christ came the whole way: 'forasmuch as the children were sharers in flesh and blood, He also in like manner partook of the same'. To redeem us God must needs express Himself in terms of our common human experiences. And the human reality of Jesus is the historic implication and the living vindication of this necessity.

From the point of view of us men and our salvation the reality and integrity of the humanity of Jesus is of vital concern. He alone can act with God for men who speaks from man's side. It is as He became our fellow, moving in a true humanity through obedience, conflict and death, that He entered into our conditions fully and availed on our behalf to receive from God's hand the suffering in which is expressed the Divine judgement upon man's sin. Thus in Him has Divine Grace become humanized; in Him, because He is total man. In the fourth century Gregory of Nazianzus repudiated the abridged humanity of the Christ of Apollinarius with the observation that that which is unassumed is unhealed. If only half Adam fell, he argues, then that which Christ assumes and saves must be half also; but if the whole of his nature fell it must be united to the whole nature of Him who was begotten and so be complete as a whole. Let them not begrudge us, he concludes, our complete salvation and clothe the Saviour with bones and nerves and the portraiture of humanity.

In this connection the declaration that judgement is committed to the Son of Man (John 5. 22) is profoundly significant. Whatever else of deeper truth there may be in it, there is this; that the sinner needs to feel the identification of his judge with himself by the possession of a common nature. When the Judge knows both the persistency and the depth of sin on the one hand, and the weakness and temptations of man on the other, then only will he be assured that the proffered forgiveness is for him. For believers the higher idea of God's goodness is made sure by the greatness of the condescension involved in His 'becoming flesh'.

THE BEGINNING OF HIS HUMAN LIFE

There is an exquisite tenderness about the record of the birth of Jesus. There is no straining, no explaining, no taking away from the 'naturalness' of the event. The delicacy of the occasion is given with singular appropriateness, a fact which marks the account with the stamp of authenticity. The circumstances are stated only in so far as they give point to the essential fact that by Mary a child was born. To the mother and those who were soon at the scene, there was no uncertainty; there was the human reality—a new life had made its appearance in the world. Luther's famous carol makes the claim that the little Lord Jesus, no crying doth make. But we cannot be so sure. At all events, of this we are certain, that all that is essentially human in an infant life was here in Him. A child is born; there is nothing more human than that. Jesus, it is made clear, was man truly; but we shall have to show later that He was not man only.

More than man, as we shall see, He was—the God-man indeed; thus human as that birth was it will have an aspect other than the human. We must therefore look again at what came to pass in Bethlehem. A child was born, that is natural; a Son was given, that is divine (Luke 1. 35 cf. Matt. 1. 20-23). God comes to man, and as man He comes. He comes as every man comes, born as a babe, and Mary of Nazareth is the chosen of God for an event which is more than human. Most fitting, then, is the creedal statement which has its grounds and warrant in the inspired records of the Incarnation of God in the birth of Jesus, 'conceived of the Holy Ghost and born of the Virgin Mary'. We cannot enter here into questions of textual criticism, but it is certainly important to underscore that we have two undoubtable genuine independent witnesses of the apostolic age to the declaration of the creed in Matt. 1. 16-25 and Luke 1. 26-38. And quite definitely must it be emphasised that no convincing explanation of the origin of the idea of the Virgin Birth has ever been put forward by those who reject the historicity of the records and the actuality of the event.

The authority of Matthew and Luke on the subject

of the Virgin Birth is unimpeachable. And they both are in accord as to the fact that the birth of Jesus was the result of a special operation of the Holy Spirit. It is beside the point to argue that because the other writers of the New Testament are silent concerning the Virgin Birth it must be regarded as doubtful. No reliable conclusion can be based upon the argument from silence. Must every New Testament writer authenticate a fact before it can be accepted? It is, of course, altogether false to suggest that because Mark and Paul give no specific declaration of their knowledge of the fact that they must therefore have been entirely ignorant of it. It was clearly not Mark's purpose to narrate the birth of Jesus. His object was rather to set down certain events of Christ's ministry within the limits of the common apostolic tradition, which began with the baptism of John, when Jesus was thirty years old, and which ended with His being 'taken up'. The omission of reference is due to design not to ignorance; it cannot be taken as in any way a contradiction of Christ's miraculous birth.

The book of Acts does not mention the circumstances of Christ's birth. Yet we know that its author, Luke, knew of it. His reliability and fidelity to his sources find confirmation by this very fact. He does not put into the mouth of the preachers of the primitive Church a belief which he would have them affirm, and about which some of them could not have been as yet aware. The silence of the New Testament can well be understood from the circumstances of the event. It is not likely that Joseph and Mary would talk of their peculiar experience in Nazareth and especially with other children about the home. It would be only as the truth of the birth became knowledge to the Church would the appropriateness of the manner of it to the Incarnation of the Son of God be appreciated. And even then the focus would be on the central fact that by the operation of the Holy Spirit there was brought upon the stage of human history One whose coming concerned man's salvation. The tendency was, as it indeed should be, to centre interest upon the essential reality; to lose sight of the human channel by giving attention to the result (cf. Gal. 4. 4; Titus 2. 11; 1 John 3. 5, 8). The truth of the matter is therefore that the doctrine of the Virgin Birth is integral to gospel faith. It was not a hypothesis suggested by man, but a fact declared by God. Put quite specifically it was a fact first, and a doctrine afterwards. When the full truth about Christ is understood, the birth as at once both human and divine will be found to be in line with the whole saving revelation of the New Testament disclosure. The Virgin Birth is not, therefore, a discovery of faith but a disclosure to faith.

It is in this way we must read Paul's statement in Phil. 2. 6-8. He is sure that in the Person of Christ there is an actual intrusion of Deity into human actuality. He who was originally in the form of God held not on to His equality with God as a prize to be grasped at, but emptied Himself, taking the form of a bond-servant and being found in fashion as a man He humbled Himself. What is this language of the apostle's but a high doctrinal statement of the historic fact of the Incarnation by supernatural conception and birth which Matthew and Luke record?

It should, however, be noted that there are passages outside the records of the first and third Gospels which may be read as alluding to Christ's miraculous entry upon the human scene; for example John 1. 13-14; 6. 42; 8. 41; Rom. 13. 4 (cf. with Luke 1. 35), Gal. 4. 4.

There is no basis for the assertion that the Christian doctrine of Christ's Person and the Christian experience of Christ's work have no stake in the assurance of His miraculous conception. The conviction of Christ's absolute worth is closely bound up with the confession of the truth of the Evangelical records concerning His coming into the world. No one can read the narratives of the birth and go away with the impression that the miraculous conception stands by itself as a sort of isolated marvel. It is rather the ground upon which the whole spiritual and ethical significance of Christ's personality rests. It is therefore apposite to note the results which follow from the declaration of His unique birth in each Gospel. After the angel's word to Joseph that he is to take Mary as his wife without fear for she is with child through the Holy Spirit, there comes the great gospel meaning of the event: Thou shalt call His name Jesus for He shall save His people from their sins. The One born in this miraculous way is the Saviour (Matt. 1. 21). Luke relates the miraculous birth to His divine Sonship (Luke 1. 35). The miraculous birth is therefore a guarantee to us that there must be some high and holy purpose in the advent of such a One. A naturalistic Christ does not require a supernatural origin. Whereas congruous with the essential heart and meaning of Christianity is the supernatural birth of One who is at once man's Saviour and God's Son.

Nor is the miraculous birth quite remote from Christian experience. There is a certain parallel between His birth physically and ours spiritually. He, and He alone, is the One who needed no second birth. He is the only accepted 'once born' among men. In His birth there was a union of the Divine Son of God with human flesh. In our spiritual new birth we are made partakers of the divine nature (2 Pet. 1. 4). His physical birth was by the agency of the Holy Ghost, as is our spiritual birth.

There is, then, a parallel between His birth in the flesh and ours in the spirit; a parallel which extends to the medium and the manifestation of it in both cases. He was conceived by the Holy Ghost and came forth a new creation of God's hand. If any man be in Christ there is a new creation—a birth from above. With His birth there was brought about a new beginning; the commencement of a new era. The old age had passed. Thus is man's spiritual birth of the Spirit—the 'before Christ' life in the flesh, and the new 'anno domini' life in the Spirit.

The birth of Christ was a miracle. The One who has experience of the miracle of the 'new birth' will not lightly dismiss the narratives of Christ's supernatural conception. Regarded systematically, seized emotionally, read in the light of our own individual experience of redemption, no language can so adequately and correctly set forth the infinite wonder, the ineffable emotion and glory as that which we find in the gospel story. Wherever Christ is born there is a miracle: a miraculous conception. The birth manifested Him forth in the world as Son of the Most High. He was, of course, uniquely Son of God. But there is a parallel; for by our spiritual new birth we are accepted as sons of God—as sons in His Sonship—'by adoption and grace' (cf. Gal. 4. 5; Eph. 1. 5; Rom. 3. 14; 5. 2; 11. 6 etc.). The birth of Jesus was the occasion for joy and envy. The drums of dawn were struck by the heralding angels and the hatred of Herod was released. A struggle had begun for supremacy between the spirit of the old and the spirit of the new.

Further Reading:
James Orr, *The Virgin Birth of Jesus* (London, 1914).
J. Gresham Machen, *The Virgin Birth of Christ* (London 1930).

Chapter Two

THE DEVELOPMENT OF HIS TRUE HUMANITY

HIS GROWTH TOWARDS MANHOOD

Jesus did not come into the world as a fully fashioned Saviour. He must needs, as the Epistle to the Hebrews makes clear, enter more deeply into our human ways and become wholly identified with our human experiences. He must show Himself, indeed, as the real and the true man. It is to the Hebrew Epistle that we owe the phrase 'in the days of His flesh' (5. 7). Although the phrase hints at His existence in 'prior days' when flesh was not His native sphere, it is one of the purposes of the writer earnestly to contend for His real and true humanity. 'This man', says the Epistle thrice over (3. 3; 7. 24; 10. 12). The writer is well assured that Jesus was an historical person who lived, sorrowed and suffered. The Son of God has come and as man partook of flesh and blood (2. 14, 16). He is thus the 'Brother' who, like His brethren, depends upon God (2. 11-13). He grew and learned in consequence of His earthly experiences (cf. 12. 2, 3). The fact of His obedience and suffering (2. 9-10; 5. 8; 10. 5), of His temptations and sympathy (2. 18; 4. 15), of His humility (5. 5) is underscored. Son though He was yet learned He obedience through the things that He suffered (5. 8). What is true of Him according to the Epistle to the Hebrews, we are to see in the Gospels' presentation of Jesus on the human level:

a personality creating its own form by a series of acts accomplishing required duty, renouncing evil's allurements and surmounting moral crises. What we see is the enlarging life of One developing full manhood. True He became neither Son nor the Sinless One, and His growth was in His vocation more properly than in His position, or even in His character; nevertheless there was a real growth in insight, in grasp of the work He had come to do. His was not the increase of moral nature but the progressive mastery of His moral vocation, in the developing matching of Himself to the growing awareness of His purpose as incarnated Saviour.

This picture of Jesus is the way the silent years spent in Galilee must be interpreted. Galilee provided Him with a home wherein to develop; Judaea with a Cross upon which to die. Thirty years passed in comparative obscurity in the carpenter's home in Nazareth, there increasing in learning, living and loving. The period has been described as that of His true and full human development. This involved outward submission to man and inward submission to God, with the attendant results of wisdom, grace and favour. The quiet years were for Him more than the time of preparation for His work, they were in a deeper sense the commencement of it. Needed for us were these thirty years of human life, that the overpowering of His divinity might not overshadow His humanity.

Only the merest glance is given of what was going on throughout those silent years in the life and experience of Jesus. But we have enough to show Him to us as 'this man'. There is a general statement of His human development and a specific reference to His awareness of His filial consciousness.

Jesus 'grew, and waxed strong, filled with wisdom; and the grace of God was upon Him ... advanced in wisdom and stature, and in favour with God and man'

(Luke 2. 40; 52). There is no crowding of the record with silly fables of arbitrary omnipotence and magical omniscience, characteristic of the Apocryphal gospels. The inspired account presents Him to us as increasing in spirit, mind and body—quietly developing during the silent years.

The account of His visit to the temple presents Him, too, as a growing boy alive to the concerns of religion (Luke 2. 41-50). Critics whose business it is to make Him less than He is, produce instances of precocious Jewish youths asking troublesome questions of the Doctors. But such instances only serve to make evident how 'natural' He was in His boyhood. It may however be observed that if there was nothing singular in the presence of a questioning youth among the doctors, yet those who heard Him were amazed at His insight and answers. But the story does not end there; there is the account of His reply to His mother which shows that He realized His relationship with God as His Father, and He Himself as under the irresistible necessity of being about His business (Luke 2. 49).

Important, therefore, were the silent years for Him in His human relation to us; and for us in our spiritual relation to Him. Spiritual babes must grow; and after the pattern of His development. Those Galilean years were for Him the period of growth. There life came upon Him—temptations were met day by day, and defeated. Clearer in its strength and vision grew His heart, to be met by the rebuffs of others and the shame of defeat and sin in those He loved. He learned how to match Himself to life's growing demands. And so it should be for us all. Those years were, too, years of obedience. Obedience to the purpose of God became His meat and drink even then. This also we should know that it is not the passing of the years that matures life, but our obedience. Those long years of silence were days of learning and discovery. What things He found out about Himself and the world during those undetailed years! What things can be discovered by those who are born anew into His world! Those thirty years were no less a period of discipline. Even then He did not do as He wished; and all through He was becoming aware that He was in a time of testing. He underwent restrictions with a willing spirit. He had to face the jeers and misunderstanding of His brothers. As He grew the division between them and Himself was becoming more clear-cut; the cleavage wider; and yet He will love them still. Thus He developed through the years to emerge for His appointed task a real and true man.

HIS MATURITY AS MAN

'The chief end of man' declares the Westminster catechism 'is to glorify God and enjoy Him for ever'. Only the one who fulfils this high purpose is real and true man. It is precisely here we see the maturity of Jesus's manhood. He is above all others the man for God, fulfilling 'man's chief end' in glorifying God.

The fulfilment of this chief end as man in glorifying God involved two necessities: the meeting of every demand of righteousness and the resisting of every approach of evil. In this respect the Baptism and the Temptations are important. In the Baptism He publicly does what throughout He has always done—fulfils all righteousness. At the Temptations He does anew what He has always done—resists all evil. There is, of course, more in the two experiences for Him than we can ever fathom. But this we know, that His Baptism was important and His Temptations real. In both He revealed Himself as the Man who made it His chief end to glorify God. And in both experiences He will reveal that which is an essential reality about Him: that He is true and real man—the mature Man.

The baptism in the Jordan (Matt. 3. 13-17; Mark 1. 7-11; Luke 3. 21-23; John 1. 29-33) is the act of Jesus's maturity. He is about to take up His life's work and in this way He makes a public avowal of His soul's intention. Here He gathers up His life and offers it in a full consecration. Jesus showed His real and true humanity by submitting to John's baptism, thus 'fulfilling all righteousness'. 'The Head was content to enter by the same gateway as the members to His specific vocation in the service of the kingdom.' In His act of baptism Jesus gave vivid expression of His identification with humanity. He identifies Himself with the people who had come to Jordan confessing their sins. He will publicly renounce the sin which He has always renounced in deed and spirit. At the Jordan He openly unites Himself with human sin; at Calvary He will openly atone for it. As man He takes His place with sinful humanity and goes forth to His task with the seal of God's approval and acknowledgement upon Him. He has been dedicated to His work in the baptismal waters and anointed with the Spirit for the fulfilment of it.

Of course, if He is more than man that, too, will have its authentication. And indeed it has—the voice from the excellent glory gave the verdict: 'This is my beloved Son in whom I am well pleased' (Matt. 3. 16, 17). This rules out any adoptionist view of Christ's Deity. The Deity of Jesus is neither that of an indwelt or a vindicated man. While the heavenly voice confirms His authentic Sonship, His own obedience in baptism assures His authentic manhood.

It is part of the evidence of man's maturity that He should have faced and fought temptation: that he should have learned to deal with the subtleties and stratagems of the devil. In the record of the Temptations we see this supreme fact demonstrated in the life of Jesus. Doubtless this was not the first encounter with Satan, nor shall it be His last. For as Luther has characteristically remarked: 'Jesus had to work hard to keep Satan at bay'. All the way along will Jesus defeat Satan and destroy him at length. But in the 'Temptations' we see him focusing his utmost attack. The time and the place—after the Dove the devil—after the waters the wilderness—are psychologically appropriate, devilishly fitting. The ecstasy of a great spiritual experience is usually succeeded by the severity of the devil's power.

Jesus had, during the silent years, come to maturity in stature, in wisdom and in favour with God and man. The devil will assail this very maturity. The stages of the temptations typify the whole round of satanic assault on man through body, mind, and spirit (cf. Luke 4. 4; I John 2. 16). Here we have focused the total score of messianic temptations. Failing to conquer in the wilderness the devil left Him for a season, as after the storm comes the calm (Luke 4. 13). But He will return with the same temptations; for there are no more—'the devil completed every temptation'. What He had resisted in the wilderness Jesus will resist again in the crush of daily life and on the Cross of suffering. The same temptations will be renewed—to be king because He has supplied bread: to come down from the Cross to induce belief. The same temptations to take the short-cut it will be; to avoid suffering, to gratify the sign-seekers, to accept worldly kingship. Gathered into the one terrible ordeal in the wilderness were all the assaults of the tempter, to satisfy His bodily cravings, to use His own wisdom to initiate the kingdom and to presume on the care of God. Make these stones 'bread'—the word had an immediate appeal to a hungry man. Esau of old sold his birthright for a pot of porridge. Jesus will meet the same temptation; but He will not sell His. He will answer satan's suggestion with 'Man shall not live by

bread alone, but by every word of God' (Matt. 4. 4;
Luke 4. 4; cf. Deut. 8. 3), for He, too, is man who has
made it His chief end to glorify God. The devil to be
sure showed Him an easy way out of His circumstances—
and into his clutches. It was so simple, so natural; just
satisfy your bodily appetites. Be selfish!

The second temptation (following Luke's account)
is the call to avoid the Cross and to assure Himself of
victory. A treaty with the devil will guarantee a triumph
over the world. Be successful!

The third temptation turned on the suggestion that
He might glorify God by some dazzling feat: casting
Himself from the temple pinnacle and thereby mesmer-
ize the masses into belief. It was the temptation to do
God's work in His own way; on His own account to do
some great thing. Be spectacular!

But He was unmoved by each approach. The devil
left Him and angels came to minister unto Him. For it is
always our affinities after temptation which prove
whether we have triumphed or not. Jesus was thus
tempted. As man He was tempted; and as man He
triumphed. There was no play-acting here. This was no
sham fight. He felt the stress of the struggle of resistance.
There was no escape for Him from the temptations which
assail mankind. He who 'in all things' was made like
unto His brethren will be 'in all points tempted like as
we are'. The 'in all things' of Hebrews 2. 17 is followed
by the 'in all points' of Hebrews 4. 15. The question is
not whether it was possible for Him to sin, or even
whether it were possible for Him not to sin. The
question is did He who encountered the devil as man
come out of the wilderness in full victory? The answer
to that is clear and unequivocal: He did.

He who had shown Himself to fulfil all righteousness
now shows Himself to resist all temptations. And it must
be well marked that He had no secret weapon. He did not

call on special means to overcome the devil other than those at the disposal of us all. By the Spirit He was led into the wilderness—in the conflict He used the Sword of the Spirit which is the Word of God (Eph. 6. 17). That was all He used; and that was enough.

Thus matured and thus assured He went forth to His ordained task to be for us the one Mediator between God and man, the Man Christ Jesus.

Further Reading:

A. Edersheim, *The Life and Times of Jesus the Messiah*, Vol. 1, Bk. II, ch. xii; Bk. III, chi. i, (London, 1886).

H. J. C. Knight, *The Temptation of our Lord* (London, 1922).

B. B. Warfield, 'The Emotional Life of our Lord', *The Person and Work of Christ*, pp. 93-145.

MAN UNDER THE SPIRIT

The references just made to the action of the Spirit in His birth, baptism and temptations, raises the question of the place of the Spirit in the life and ministry of Jesus. It seems clear that Jesus experienced an indwelling of the Spirit for the perfecting of His life as man and an enduement of the Spirit for the fulfilment of His office as Messiah. The effects of the Spirit were, that is to say, both personal and ministerial.

It is declared in John 3. 34 that the Spirit was given to Him 'without measure'. True enough the words 'unto Him' do not occur in the original Greek, but the arguments that they should be presupposed are overwhelming. All that was necessary for Him by virtue of His human nature to possess was imparted to Him without lack by the Holy Spirit.

It is evident that the Spirit's indwelling and overshadowing went together with the development of Jesus's manhood, and were the cause of this development. Jesus needed the gift of the Holy Spirit to enable His human nature, in increasing measure, to be His instrument in the working out of His holy design. And all that He needed was bountifully supplied. Born of the

Spirit, He grew in spirit (reading pneumati: Luke 2. 40). The Spirit who secured that His human flesh, derived from Mary, should not become the basis of sin's operation, made certain also His progress in spiritual and mental development and His advance in holiness and knowledge. The Holy Spirit not only endowed the human nature of Christ with all necessary equipment, but He also caused these to be exercised, gradually, into full activity. During His days in the flesh, Jesus was under the constant and penetrating operation of the Spirit. It was as a man under the Spirit that Jesus carried out His duties in the carpenter's shop in Nazareth, and there submitted to the rule of His earthly home. He was prepared of the Spirit for the time of His showing forth and sending forth to fulfil His messianic office. In and by the Spirit He fulfilled all righteousness and resisted all temptation. and in the power of the Spirit He returned into Galilee (Luke 4. 14).

At the baptism He was consecrated for His office by the Spirit's descent in the form of a dove, the inner strengthening and equipping for the task He needed. The outward symbol was not for His sake, but that human eyes might behold the evidence of His official calling and human lips might declare what they had seen and heard. Now developed to manhood under the Spirit, He goes forth freshly anointed to His messianic work. Coming into Galilee in the power of the Spirit, in that power He will remain and under that power He will work out a life of obedient service. For the Spirit that descended upon Him at the baptism 'abode on Him' (John 1. 32).

It is important, therefore, to note our Lord's own declaration in the synagogue of Nazareth, when He took to Himself the words of Isaiah 61. 1, 'the Spirit of the Lord is upon Me', anointing Him to preach and to fulfil the messianic work of this prophetic passage (cf. Luke 4. 17). Jesus carried out every function of the messianic office in the power of the Spirit. And since the Holy Spirit is the divine executive of the mighty acts of God, it need not be thought strange that Jesus should have lived His life and fulfilled His divine mission through His power. It is, indeed, expressly stated that this is so. Jesus could neither do anything (John 5. 19, 30; 8. 28) nor speak anything (John 3. 34; 7. 18; 8. 28) of Himself. He cast out Satan by the Spirit of God (Matt. 12. 28), and declared the words of God through the same Spirit (John 3. 34). Thus the Spirit remained with Him throughout His earthly life controlling His mind, will and actions so that He learned from God, acted for God and taught of God unto the fulness of the stature of a perfect man. In the end He offered Himself through the eternal Spirit (Heb. 9. 14). Even after His resurrection, we are told it 'was through' the Holy Spirit that He gave commandment to His chosen apostles concerning His continuing purpose in the world (Acts. 1. 2). There is no strangeness, no incongruity, therefore, in Peter's sermonic declaration in the house of Cornelius that Jesus of Nazareth was anointed 'with the Holy Ghost and with power'; and with that anointing and in that power He lived a life well-pleasing to God, going about doing good (Acts 10. 38).

This intimate relation and association between Jesus and the Spirit makes fitting the biblical statement of the connection between the risen Jesus and the present Spirit. Pentecost was won for us at Calvary; thus 'having received of the Father, the promise of the Spirit, He hath poured forth this, which ye see and hear' (Acts 2. 33). None knew better than He how much His people needed the Spirit for their life and task. When, therefore, He went away, He sent the Spirit for the perfecting of the saints unto the work of the ministry (Eph. 4. 3, 4, 13 RSV).

35

Further reading on the relation of the Holy Spirit to the life
and ministry of Jesus:

George Smeaton, *The Doctrine of the Holy Spirit*, ch. 2 (London,
1961).
Lewis A. Humpheries, *The Holy Spirit in Faith and Experience*,
ch. 5 (London, 1911).
A. C. Downer, *The Mission and Ministration of the Holy
Spirit*, ch. 3 (Edinburgh, 1909).
A. Kuyper, *The Work of the Holy Spirit*, chs. xx-xxiii (Grand
Rapids, 1946).

Chapter Three

THE CHALLENGE OF HIS PERFECT HUMANITY

THE SINLESS MAN

Jesus fulfilling all righteousness and resisting all temptation—Jesus the man, at every point and at every moment of His earthly life under the Spirit—is presented in the Scriptures and confessed by the Church as the one perfect Man that the world has ever seen and known.

There were those in the early days who held the view, as we have noted, that the flesh is sinful in itself and as a consequence denied the reality of Christ's material body. The claim by some writers that Paul's teaching gave substance to such a view can be set aside. True enough, the apostle does bring sin and the flesh into close relation (cf. e.g. Rom. 6. 6; 8. 3). But he uses the term 'flesh' (sarx) in a twofold way. In the far larger number of instances it has the sense of human nature conditioned by the body. In thirty-five of the ninety-one occurrence of its usage, however, the apostle gives it an ethical significance with the meaning of human nature as conditioned by the fall. It is in this context he relates sin closely to the flesh, as for example, in his statement that 'in me, that is in my flesh, dwelleth no good thing' (Rom. 7. 18). Never, however, does Paul say that the 'flesh' is in itself sinful. It is that part of man's nature which more readily gives sin its opportunity. It is that upon which sin impinges; its basis of operation. Decisive

37

against any identification of sin with the flesh is Paul's teaching that the body can be cleansed and sanctified (1 Cor. 6. 13, 19, 20; 2 Cor. 7. 1; cf. Rom. 6. 13; 12. 1). The apostle certainly insists on the reality of Christ's body (Col. 2. 9f), and at the same time maintains His sinlessness (2 Cor. 5. 21), thus making it clear that flesh is not sinful by its very nature.

The fact is that sin is not conceived of in the Bible as a spiritual bacillus hiding in the blood of the mother and received into the veins of the child. Sin is essentially moral and spiritual, not material and tangible. The Church has always set itself against all Manichaean ideas which regard sin as identifiable with the material substance of our being. Sin is not an essential part of the stuff of manhood; it is an intruder. The more sinful a man the less of a man he is; the less sinful the more truly is he a man. Thus the sinlessness of Jesus establishes the claim to the perfection of His manhood.

On the other hand, there were those, as again we have pointed out, during the early centuries of the Church, who placed the seat of sin in the mind and therefore evacuated Christ of a human mind, which they filled with the depotentiated Divine Logos or Reason. But such a truncated humanity in the case of Christ makes pointless the biblical injunctions to believers to have the mind of Christ (cf. 1 Cor. 2. 16 (nous); Phil. 2. 5 (phroneo touto)).

The truth of the matter is, however, that the life of Jesus was distinctively and authentically human. Only in that which makes all the rest of us less than human did He differ from us. In this particular was He unique. He alone lived within our human sinful race a human sinless life. The historic records never betray any attempt to gild the lily. They do not set out to 'prove' His sinlessness. They tell the story without affectation; just as He was among men. The fact is the Synoptic Gospels make no explicit claim to moral purity on the part of Jesus. But neither do they set out to prove His innocence or to eulogise Him. They give the account of His life as He lived it; and that is enough.

Yet as we follow the record we note how He stood the tests of intimacy and enmity. His very presence was a rebuke, a cause of shame in others (cf. Matt. 3. 14; 27. 19; Luke 5. 8; 23. 47; John 19. 6).

The Jesus of the gospels knew more about sin than anyone; yet He Himself never betrayed the least consciousness of it. Sin in others He saw, He rebuked, He forgave; He grieved over it, He suffered for it; He knew what was in man yet could issue the challenge, 'Which of you convinceth me of sin?' (John 8. 46). With Him there was no memory of sin's defeat, no trace of sin's scars, no shame of a bad conscience. He lived all His days without the personal sense of sin's guilt and the personal fear of sin's consequences. The question of Mark 10. 18 cannot be taken as 'a veiled confession of moral delinquency'. In very truth the adult life of Jesus, as depicted in the Gospels, was pure from the traces of sin which means that in His case there was no derangement of nature or native sickness of soul, as with us from our beginning (cf. Luke 1. 35; Acts 3. 27, 30).

As we examine the New Testament we find overwhelming testimony to the fact that in Christ sin found no opportunity to work out its ill deeds and deserts. It is a universal saying that no man is a hero to his valet; yet, in the case of Jesus, we find those most intimate with Him and closest to Him, unable to record any blemish. John, for example, who sets down the statement that 'if we say that we have no sin we deceive ourselves' (1 John 1. 8), deliberately excludes Christ whom he knew (3. 5). Paul is no less assured that his redeeming Lord is a sinless Saviour (2 Cor. 5. 21).

The Epistle to the Hebrews, of all the New Testament writings, finds in the sinless perfection of the man Jesus the reason for a luminous contrast between the old covenant and the new (Heb. 7. 26; 9. 14). Significantly the passage of Scripture in which His equality with us as regards all temptations is expressed also emphatically exempts from it this one particular, sin (Heb. 4. 15). It was, then, evidently the certain conclusions of the apostolic writers that the life of Jesus was sinlessly holy. He not only kept Himself from all sin in deed and word; but positively, He pleased God in all requirements of human life. And these apostolic writers, it must be clear, were God's elect and providential interpreters of His saving purpose in Christ. He who was to perform so high a task they knew to be holy in the whole area of His life. This sacred conviction of theirs was not an intrusion on the revelation, but, in truth, part of the very scheme of it; for they were the conveyors of the message of God's grace, not corruptors of it.

Only a sinless person could be a channel and guarantor of the divine pardon. And if salvation is to be achieved in this Man then He, on His part, must be altogether free from the bias and taint of moral evil. The analogy, therefore, of the 'lamb without blemish' of the Old Testament must be seen as bringing the sinlessness of Jesus into direct relation with God's redemptive work. A whole series of passages showing the direct influence of Isaiah 53 unite the Servant of the Lord with the Sinless One of the Gospels to show that He, upon whom the Lord lays our iniquities, is Himself without any (cf. 1 Pet. 2. 22; see Acts 3. 13; 4. 27, 30—where for 'Child' read 'Servant' RV).

The man Jesus is then the truly normal man—the one sinless man. The remarkable fact is that it is the reality of Jesus's sinlessness which has produced throughout the history of the Church, not a claim to perfection, but the sense of imperfection in His followers. For, as has been well said, the sinful human brain is no Jupiter-head from which this sinless human figure could have emerged. In every way His life is what human life was meant to be. He loved God with His whole mind and heart and soul and strength, for His was the life of perfect worship. He fulfilled all the requirements of the blessed life, making actual those beatitudes which He taught to His disciples (Matt. 6. 3-12; cf. Luke 6. 20-23). He took a towel and demonstrated that He had taken the position of lowly service. The poem of love of I Corinthians 13 can be taken as a vivid portrait of His life of perfect love. The consecrated life of which Romans 13 is an outline found in Him incarnate reality. The conclusion, then, of the matter as regards the sinless Jesus is just this, as H. R. Mackintosh says: 'No miracle of Christ equals the miracle of His sinless life. To be holy in all thought and feeling; never to fail in duty to others, never to transgress the law of perfect love to God or man, never to exceed or to come short—this is a condition outstripping the power of imagination'.

Further reading:
C. Ullman, *The Sinlessness of Jesus* (Edinburgh, 1901).
B. B. Warfield, 'Jesus' alleged Confession of Sin', *The Person and Work of Christ*, (Philadelphia, 1950) pp. 149-185.

THE SIGNIFICANT MAN

The Figure of Jesus as it is presented to us in the Gospel story and interpreted to us in the rest of the New Testament is that of One who was no unearthly angelic visitant, no demigod in human shape. It was a real man who lived a perfect life amid the human realities of our common way. It was as man Jesus came and lived and died. It was as man He came back from the secret gloom of the sepulchre after three days. After the resurrection

He still bore the nail prints, and with the marks of the passion yet on Him they saw Him go up into Heaven. At the right hand of God is a real man glorified. Here is a comfort to faith. At the throne of God we are understood. Mercy has still a human heart and pity a human face. Christ as man stands beside God for us. He who knows our human pathway with its toils and twists still cares. He has been on our human level and understands the stuff of our human nature. He who has shared so intimately with us can sympathise with us fully.

But He is—this perfect man—the ideal of faith. The world's dream has ever been for the coming of a perfect man. The vision of the perfect man satisfies the measure of the world's ideal. What all have sought for, Christianity alone presents. And whatever surprises there may be in store for the world, Jesus will never be surpassed. He is the realization of all that is true and right, the perfection of all beauty, the crown of all character. The gospel alone holds out to the world the reality of the perfect man: perfect in body, therefore miracles leaped from His hands; perfect in mind therefore truth flowed from His lips. All men are measured by the Perfect Man.

We cannot label or level Jesus. Other men are known by the predominance of one or two characteristics. One is brave: another is kind. But in Him all blend into one glorious harmony. Qualities which would contradict each other in other men are woven together in Him. Brave beyond all, He was humble above all; a man of sorrows, yet full of joy. Fearless in unmasking sin, yet gracious with sinners.

For humanity, Jesus as the Ideal Man is at once its heartbreak and its hope. The ideal which He embodies is such that no man, strive as he will, can ever become wholly identified with it. It always sets up a contrast and a conflict within man between what he 'is' and what he 'ought to be'. Jesus the perfect man—man's ideal—thus becomes the measure of man's failure and need. It is in this way that the reading of the perfect humanity of Jesus becomes the stepping-stone to faith. The personality of Jesus pales every comparison and thus shows the futility of His being forced into the too narrow scheme of an example. As an example He is beyond human attainment. Thus, to see the perfect man as He is revealed in the pages of the gospel records is to see One who cannot finally be assessed in human categories. He truly stands alone. To be like Him is the Christian's highest hope, to meet Him the sinner's greatest dread. Jesus has no fellow, no repeat.

It was because He was real man, true man and perfect man that we must press on. Never before or since has there been such as He. In the light of His eyes is the glory of God, in the perfume of His personality the sweetness of heaven, in the kingly bearing of His manhood the majesty of the eternal, in the wounds of His body the divine marks of a love everlasting, in His strong uplifted arm the saving strength of the Godhead. Such a man must be at the same time more than man. Since He embodies an ideal which brings Him into marked contrast with the rest of men, He presents Himself as One who is more than the leader of men. He is not merely an expression of that which is inherent in humanity, but which, more significantly, is creative of human standards. What we desire is not a man who can only rouse us to troubled exertion; we have need of One who can give us peace of soul. A Christ who is nothing more than an unattainable ideal and an embodied law is not sufficient for our need. Such may be little more than a lovely picture; or, perhaps, the story of One who lived well in His day, but, alas, is no more.

The fact is, however, that one who sees Jesus as the perfect man, as humanity's ideal, will, if He looks deeply again, see Him as more; will feel the need of One who was more than perfect man in the dead past. He will need a more than perfect man in the living present. In truth we need a Christ who is alive, so that He can still help us in our weakness; and so, because of the need of our soul, we must look at Jesus again, to see whether He is not something more than merely our heartening and yet at the same time our disheartening example.

Further reading:

Otto Borchert, *The Original Jesus* (London, 1933).
James S. Stewart, *The Life and Teaching of Jesus Christ* (London 1933).
Samuel G. Craig, *Jesus of Yesterday and Today* (Philadelphia, 1956).

THE SON OF MAN

In an earlier age the title Son of Man was taken without further ado to refer to the human nature of Christ in contrast with that of Son of God, which specified His divine nature. The term 'man' in the title gave easy justification for this ready equation. There are certainly a few instances in which the use of the title does indicate reflection on Jesus's part on His human nature. There is, for example, the declaration of Mark 2. 27, 28 in which Jesus asserted that as Son of Man He is lord even of the Sabbath. The Sabbath was made for man and not man for the Sabbath. Here Jesus may be regarded as identifying Himself with the children of man and vindicating their rights as men, while at the same time indicating His supremacy above them. So, too, may it be in the passage in which He contrasts Himself with the austere preacher of the wilderness with the words, 'the Son of Man came eating and drinking' (Matt. 11. 19). Is He here suggesting His sympathy with all the natural and simple enjoyments of human life? There are those who, on the strength of such passages, still prefer to understand the title 'Son of Man' as expressive of His deep connection with humanity.

That His feeling of identity with mankind was a ruling sentiment with Him needs no demonstration. With all that is highest and holiest in man's nature and destiny He was in the fullest and profoundest sympathy. His compassion reached down to all that is most pathetic and painful in our human lot. He is without doubt the Brother of all men, and Man of men. When, however, the title is looked at more closely it will be seen that the passages which can have this undeniable reference are comparatively few. Thus the very title which holds the term 'man' will be found to present Him to us as more than man.

It is well known that the title Son of Man was Jesus's most frequent designation for Himself. He seems, indeed, to have preferred it above all others. Other names He might acknowledge, or at least not repudiate, but this name stands alone as the name that was His favourite, and as a result became in His use almost eliminative of other names, the Son of God alone excepted, though even the latter did not attain the same frequency as Son of Man upon His lips.

The title comes seventy times in the first three Gospels, and is found as early as Mark 2. 10. Although it becomes more frequent in its use towards the end of the Gospels, it is clear that it was on the lips of Jesus from the beginning of His ministry. After the great confession of Peter it appeared to gain a profounder significance with a wider public. We may set aside the view that the phrase meant no more than the simple equivalence of 'I', or that it meant merely 'the ideal man'.

Yet Jesus never defined the title nor did He indicate where He found it. It occurs frequently in the Old Testament (Ps. 8. 4; 80. 17; Ezekiel, 90 times where it refers to the prophet himself). By general consent it is believed that Daniel 7. 13 is the source of the title. There we have the vision of one like unto a Son of Man who receives a kingdom. The title occurs, too, in both the Similitudes of Enoch and Second Esdras—if the passages are indeed pre-Christian. Special interest is taken by scholars in the first of these references in which the figure of the Son of Man, who is of old and wears the aspect of a celestial being, is definite and personified. It cannot be said for certain that Jesus drew upon this circle of ideas in taking to Himself the title. The truth is, perhaps, that Jesus derived it partly from the Old Testament and partly from His own messianic consciousness.

It is significant, however, that the use of the title seems to have occasioned no surprise either on the part of Jesus's disciples or the public at large. It was quite evidently a known title, although it does not seem to have been used by the Jews for the Messiah before Jesus came. The question of the multitudes recorded in John 12. 34 concerns, not the use of the designation by Jesus, but the announcement that as Messiah He must be 'lifted up'. The juxtaposition in this passage of the term 'Messiah' and 'Son of Man' make it clear that the title by this time had acquired a messianic significance.

What, therefore, Jesus was asserting in so designating Himself was that He was in the world to fulfil a divine mission in connection with the messianic kingdom. He seems to have preferred the title to that of 'Messiah', possibly for the reason that it stood farthest removed from the Jewish prostitution of the messianic office into a military dictatorship of a this-worldly pomp. It may be conceded that the title acquired a more definite messianic connotation as Jesus became more and more able to unfold to His disciples His messianic calling and intention. It is, at any rate, significant to observe that as He the more disclosed His Messiahship so the more frequently does He use the title Son of Man. The first open admission of His messianic vocation is definitely associated with the term (Matt. 16. 13, 21f.; Mark 8. 27, 31f.; cf. Luke 9. 18, 22f.).

A consideration of the passages in which the term is found shows that it combines the two ideas of suffering and glory. There are several references where the thought of suffering is uppermost (see, for example, Mark 8. 31 (Luke 9. 22); Mark 9. 9 (Matt. 17. 9); Mark 9. 12 (Matt. 17. 12); Mark 9. 31 (Matt. 17. 22); Mark 10. 33 (Matt. 20. 18; Luke 18. 31); Mark 14. 21 (Matt. 26. 24; Luke 22. 22); Mark 14. 41; Matt. 12. 40 (Luke 11. 30); Matt. 26. 2; Luke 22. 48). Passages which show the Son of Man in the context of triumph and glory are no less numerous (see, for example, Mark 8. 38 (Luke 9. 26); Mark 13. 26 (Matt. 25. 31; Luke 21. 27); Mark 14. 62 (Matt. 26. 64); Luke 22. 29; Matt. 13. 14; 16. 27, 28; 24. 27; (Luke 17. 24); Matt. 24. 37, 39 (Luke 17. 26); Matt. 24. 44 (Luke 12. 40); Luke 12. 8; 17. 22, 30; 18. 8; 21. 36).

Seen, therefore, according to the distribution of its use and the contexts in which it occurs it becomes certain that Jesus took the title as stating His oneness with human kind as real, representative and typical Man. But with this oneness with man, there goes into the term the thought of His uniqueness in humanity, by appointment to future glory and transcendent sway. This primary significance was enriched, especially towards the closing days of Jesus's ministry, with the added thought of suffering. Humanity and apocalyptic triumph in the future thus combine to make the term Son of Man one of supreme interest and importance. Jesus called Himself Son of Man against the background of Daniel 7.13 which has reference to a kingdom; and it was as founder of the Kingdom of God that He came like unto a son of man. The Son of Man must suffer . . . when the Son of Man comes in His glory; here unite the ideas of suffering and sovereignty. The humiliation is offset by the exaltation. The King comes to the throne by way of the Cross. Humility and majesty meet and blend in the character and experience of this Son of Man.

The dozen or so references in John's Gospel reflect a theology which not only presupposes, but also amplifies the messianic significance of the title for the personality of the incarnate Christ. Primarily the element of supernatural pre-existence is emphasised (3. 13, etc.).

The two groups into which the term falls correspond to the Old Testament representations of the Messiah. On the one side there is His lowliness as the Servant of Jehovah, and on the other His lordship as God's Viceregent. In the Old Testament these two lines of prophetic anticipation never meet. It is in Jesus that the problem of their remarkable contrast finds its solution. Thus the term Son of Man at once revealed and concealed the glory of a Messiah who suffers, and the humility of a King who reigns.

Further reading:
Geerhardus Vos, *The Self-disclosure of Jesus*, ch. x (Grand Rapids, 1954).
E. G. Jay, *Son of Man, Son of God*, (London, 1965).

THE DIVINE REALITY

Whom do men say that I the Son of Man am?

Chapter Four

THE TRUTH AS IT IS REVEALED

It was at Caesarea Philippi that Jesus put His revealing questions to His disciples (Matt. 16. 13f.; cf. Mark 8. 27f.; Luke 9. 18f.). The place, the time and the persons concerned were all significant. The town of Caesarea Philippi, nestling at the base of Mount Hermon, was beyond the direct influence of the Jews. With His eyes towards the great beyond of the Gentile world, Jesus asked the question which centred upon the meaning of His own Person. Caesarea Philippi was so called by Philip the tetrarch, who shrewdly and diplomatically associated his own name with that of Caesarea Augustus. But neither Philip nor Augustus has left his name to the ages in the significant and saving way than did the One who stood there that day with His fishermen friends. It was He, not they, who turned the course of the centuries. Whom do men say that I the Son of Man am? The question receives a new meaningfulness in the light of the events of history.

The timing, too, was important. The impending denouement was at hand. Jesus opens the way to put the most searching and the most momentously important question to His disciples (Matt. 16. 15). Their attitude towards Him must be openly revealed. They must be made to commit themselves. Jesus will have them state first what 'the people' think of Him. He is not concerned to ask about the opinion of the rulers. He knows only too well that they are blind to the ultimate facts of who He is. But the people—they know His miracles, have heard His teaching, have rejoiced to see His day; have they gone further? Have they attained to a glimmer of understanding of His person and mission? The various notions of the crowd are chronicled by the disciples (Matt. 16. 14).

What of the disciples themselves? He employed the term Son of Man in the question He asked concerning the views of His people. But have they seen anything of the hidden glory in the man of Galilee? Have they discovered anything of the majesty which shone through the humanity? Inevitably Peter, 'the coryphaeus of the Apostle choir', speaks. He makes the great confession: 'Thou art the Christ' (Luke), 'the Son of the living God' adds Matthew. Some have asserted that the added words of Matthew are a mere expansion probably inserted to off-set the term 'Son of Man'. The suggestion is itself improbable. The words in Matthew's record express the simple yet profound truth about Jesus. The contrast, if one must be sought, is really with what follows: 'Blessed art thou Simon, son of John, for flesh and blood hath not revealed this unto you, but my Father in Heaven'. The use of the phrase 'my Father' in Christ's words instead of 'God' suggests that the divine disclosure that had been made to Peter had reference to the fact of the paternal and filial relationship between God and Jesus. The verb used for 'hath revealed' is reminiscent of Matthew 11. 27, where the unique knowledge by the Father of the Son and the Son of the Father, as well as the exclusive work of the One to reveal the Other, are declared. In Peter's declaration we have a concrete example of the revelation of the unique Sonship of Jesus. The contrast is, therefore, between Simon son of John, who knew himself to have a human father, and 'the Son of the living God'; as

Jesus immediately refers to God as 'my Father' for He knew no human one. Peter's faith-declaration was the result of no human insight, the discovery of no earthly wisdom. It was given from above (cf. Matt. 11. 28; Luke 10. 22). John, too, can recall that this was his experience. In no less a revelatory manner did he know the truth about Christ. We, he says, speaking of himself and maybe including others with him—'We beheld His glory, the glory as of the only begotten of the Father, full of grace and truth' (John 1. 14).

The episode of the great confession at Caesarea Philippi is evidently of great import. More especially must be marked the double fact that here Jesus openly accepted the acknowledgement of His Messiahship and clearly asserted a unique Father-Son relationship between God and Himself. Quite without doubt, then, Jesus regarded Himself as having His ultimate place on the divine side of reality.

This brings us face to face with what has been called the 'Great Dilemma'. Jesus has stood the tests of the intimacy of friendship and the scrutiny of enemies as being utterly true. Can, therefore, the impression that He generates, that He cannot be understood fully in human terms, be set aside? He has shown Himself as perfect Man, but does He speak falsely in His claims to be more than man? He has lived under the Spirit of God, can it then be possible that He should blasphemously assert an unclouded openness of His mind to the Father as the very essence of His being, if it were not so? It just cannot be possible.

He was the Truth, but He was hounded to death for speaking falsehood. He fulfilled the law, yet they regarded Him as the supreme law-breaker. He was hailed as King, but condemned as a traitor. He worked what those who experienced His miracles knew to be the works of God, but is to be found standing trial as a sorcerer. He forgave sins only to be charged with being an imposter. He took the place of God and demonstrated His Godhood in many ways, openly and obliquely, but they took Him for a blasphemer. But can He who exemplified every virtue be held to have none? Can the One who dooms all by His shining presence be the disgrace of all with an unholy disregard for all that is true, and good, and lovely, and pure? We have not so learned Christ. He must be what He claimed Himself to be; what in very truth He Himself lived as being true. Jesus demonstrated God; illustrated God. Jesus gave God His right name; and Christian experience discovers Jesus as the right place to meet God. The Christian finds in Jesus, not simply a high doctrine of God or an inspiring faith in God, but the very life and power which are of God Himself. In Christ He finds all he looks for in God. Jesus Christ is all that God can be to us and does all that God can do for us. Here is no mere pattern of godlikeness, but the incarnation of Godhood. We find God in Christ, not beyond Him. To speak of Him in terms of perfect man and man under the Spirit, is to speak of Him truly; but not adequately and not finally—in these terms.

Jesus appears then to belong to the divine side of reality. He is of God, from God, for God. But in what precise sense is this to be understood and on what authority does it rest?

Thus dual question will find its answer as the facts are investigated, first by looking at Christ's own claims concerning Himself, and then at the biblical teaching regarding Him.

THE SELF-MANIFESTATION OF CHRIST AS TO HIS DEITY

We cannot in the space we have, deal in any exhaustive way with all the ideas and questions here involved. All we can do is to indicate the lines along which the subject may be approached. There are three broad facts which must be taken into account in connection with Christ's self-attestation to His divineness. Note must be made of His self-consciousness, His self-assertion, and His self-disclosure as needing a higher reference than that of even a sinless man and a man Spirit-controlled for its understanding.

(i) The evidence shows that Christ knew Himself to be uniquely related to God from the beginning. He spoke in the most intimate way of God as His Father and in the most personal way of God as '*my* Father'. The significance of this is given further implication when it is recalled that Jesus designates God as 'Holy Father' (John 17. 11). He regarded Himself as standing in a special relationship with Him to whom He refers as the Lord of heaven and earth (Matt. 11. 25). He links Himself with God in the intimate 'We' of a unique association—'We', both of us, the Father and the Son (John 14. 23). This filial consciousness was the constant factor in all of His earthly life. The disciples saw Him most certainly at the beginning as a man specially anointed with the Spirit for some divine purpose which they came to learn was His messianic vocation. But for Jesus Himself the more fundamental fact was that of His divine origin. At the age of twelve He used the words 'my Father' with no less intimacy and significance than He did in the Upper Room. And those words used during that early visit to the temple betray a naturalness which makes it sure that He was then fully aware of Himself as specially associated with His Father in heaven. This was not the moment of His becoming conscious of His Sonship.

Jesus, as we have seen, is presented in the Gospels as a man under the Spirit. But it is important to emphasise that there is no casual connection to be traced between the Spirit-baptism and His Sonship. He did not become a

Son as a consequence of His receiving the Spirit. The truth is rather that He was baptised with the Spirit because He was already Son. The coming of the Spirit relates to His messianic vocation, not to His Sonship. It is by reason of His Sonship He is qualified by nature for the fulfilling of His office of Messiah. As Messiah He is called to act in close affiliation with God. He is God's absolute representative. Such a purpose and position presuppose a deep and profound oneness of nature that only One who is in the highest sense Son could adequately fulfil. The office of Messiahship calls for One who is truly Son. On the other hand, because of His Sonship a high type of Messiahship must follow. The high office requires a high Person; while the high Person will only fulfil an office commensurate with His character and dignity. Thus at the Baptism His Sonship was attested by the Father, while in the Temptations His Sonship was assailed by the devil.

When we take into account how strict and exact Jesus was in His utterances (cf. Matt. 5. 34, 37; 12. 36), and how He Himself placed limits consonant with His incarnate state to His actions (Matt. 20. 23), and to His knowledge (Matt. 24. 36), then we see how utterly certain He was in the enduring consciousness of His filial relationship with God. Jesus was aware that the Sonship He knew was no mere phase of His earthly existence. He regarded Himself as having being the object of the divine love before ever the earth was. He brought His Sonship with Him from heaven (John 6. 38, 46, 62; 8. 23, 42). In the depths of His own consciousness there was the continued prescience of His divine origin. For Him it was natural to regard the proper ending of His life on earth, when His work is done, as a return to the glory which was His in a prior existence (John 14. 12, 28; 16. 10).

(ii) From the discussion of what Jesus knew Himself

to be, we turn to note what He declared Himself to be. Here we see that His self-testimony is consistent with His self-consciousness. The claims made by Jesus, directly and indirectly, are astonishing in their implications. Yet they are not obviously excessive; they somehow ring true.

So much could be said here that we can only allow ourselves the barest chronicle of the facts; and not then of them all.

Some of Jesus's direct claims put Him without question on God's side. He declared His Sonship with God as His Father, which those who heard understood as being an assertion of equality with God (John 5. 18). This very equality with God He unhesitatingly maintained (John 10. 30). The honour due to God He regarded as due to Himself (John 5. 22, 23).

There are important passages in which Jesus makes astounding claims which begin with the phrase 'I Am'. This phrase has a backward glance to the Old Testament and suggests that Jesus was in this oblique way identifying Himself with the Jehovah Great I Am, of Exodus 3. 14. The declarations themselves relate broadly to what Jesus can claim to be in Himself—for example, 'I am the way, the truth and the life'; 'I am the resurrection and the life' and the like. Life is a Godlike thing; it cannot be maintained and understood apart from God. Jesus asserts that His is the prerogative to give life—'even so the Son' (John 5. 21). All life, both physical and spiritual, is because of Him (cf. John 1. 3; see Col. 1. 16, 17; Heb. 1. 2).

Other 'I Am' statements make the claim that Jesus can be and do for men what God alone can be and do for them. 'I am the true bread'; 'I am the good Shepherd'. This last claim is specially significant because it makes the Jesus of the New Testament to be to His people the same as the Jehovah of the Old Testament (cf. Ps. 23.

4; Isa. 40. 10, 11; Ezek. 34. 11, 12, 18—compare with John 10. 1f).

Throughout the Gospels Jesus is found calling men to service and sacrifice, even unto death 'for His sake'. This is a bold demand; but it is enhanced and becomes credible when it is remembered that in the Old Testament the prophet and the psalmist reinforce their messages with the words 'for the Lord's sake', or more usually 'for His name's sake'. By deliberately substituting 'for my sake' Jesus was clearly putting Himself in the place of God.

Over and over again we find Jesus making assertions which do not come to us as exaggerated, unreal or absurd. They have about them the quiet certainty of a divine authority. He will build His Church and no opposition will frustrate His purpose (Matt. 16. 18). To confess His name is to be blessed of Him and to be accepted of His Father in heaven (Matt. 10. 32, 33; Luke 12. 8, 9). He identified the word and will of God with His own word and will (Luke 6. 46-49; 11. 28; Matt. 7. 21-29; 12. 49, 50). He asserted in His own name as authoritative a new commandment (Matt. 5. 43 f.: Luke 6. 37 f.:). His use of the expression, 'Verily I say unto you', was a deliberate substitution for the prophetic 'Thus saith the Lord'. Thus can He speak in His own name the things which be of God. The prophets spake *for* God; He will speak *as* God.

Jesus presented Himself throughout the Gospels not first as a prophet but as the subject of all prophecy. No prophet ever dared to make himself not merely *a* but *the* subject not only of his own prophecy but equally of that of others. But this was assumed and asserted in the case of Christ (cf. Matt. 1. 22; 26. 24; Luke 18. 31; 24. 25-27). Jesus made soteriological and eschatological claims of the highest order. He had come, He maintained, to give His life a ransom for many (Matt. 20. 28; cf.

Mark 10. 45). His body broken and His blood shed are for man's salvation (Matt. 26. 26f.). He must die, but He will rise again (Matt. 16. 21; 17. 9, 23; Luke 13. 32; John 10. 18). To Me, He declares, has all power been given (Mt. 28. 18), and He will come again (John 14. 3, 18, 23 etc.).

Particular note should be taken of the passage in which Jesus illustrates in His claim what may be taken as a fundamental theological dictum, that only by God can God be known. This 'embryonic Fourth Gospel' statement, as P. T. Forsyth calls it, of Matthew 11. 27 (Luke 10. 22), makes the dictum sure. For in their ultimate relationship and being, no one knows the Son except the Father, and the Father except the Son. Man's relation to Him assures his destiny, and in the end it is by Him he is judged.

(iii) It remains just to add a few words on the third aspect of the present subject: the self-disclosure of Christ, what He showed Himself to be.

Here it should be observed that Jesus showed a knowledge that was unique and a power that was divine.

We have noted how Jesus was truly human and how He grew in wisdom and knowledge. He who asked questions in the temple at the age of twelve continued to do so throughout His earthly life (cf. Mark 9. 5; Luke 18. 41; 24. 17; John 11. 34 etc.). Doubtless many of His enquiries were simply a means of beginning a conversation. At the same time He evidently sought information on occasions. And some at least of His inquiries were sincerely for this purpose.

On the other hand, it is clear that parallel with this there must be set the other fact, that being more than man He exhibited a knowledge beyond the human. It was a conviction with His disciples, gained through their experience with Him, that He knew all things (cf. John 2. 25; 16. 30; 21. 17). And this conviction

59

was born in them out of the fact of His own self-disclosure. He demonstrated that He did indeed know
what was in man and needeth not that any should tell
Him (John 2. 25). He saw the true heart of Nathanael
(John 1. 47) and of Peter (John 1. 42), and of the eager
young ruler (Mark 10. 21), and of the woman who was a
sinner (Luke 7. 37f.), and of His opponents (Matt.
12. 25; Mark 2. 8). Instances such as these could be
multiplied, and others added, to show that the knowledge
of Jesus extended to external matters, although always in
the service of His moral purpose (cf. John 1. 50; 4.
39; 6. 70; cf. Luke 5. 10).

It would seem, therefore, that from the twofold
nature of the one Christ of the Gospels, there follows a
twofold knowledge. He knew men as their Lord and as
their Brother. Being God He knows men from a distance,
as it were. He holds the key of their being. He knoweth
our thoughts afar off. Being man He knows men at close
quarters. He has journied along our pathway. Peter gave
expression to this penetrating and perfect knowledge of
his life by Christ when he said to Him: 'Thou knowest
all things' (oidas—by the fact of Who you are), 'thou
knowest that I love Thee (ginoskeis—by your experience
of me (John 21. 17)).

'Man is a great deep' says Augustine; yet Jesus knows
what is in man. It is this fact of His knowledge which
gives reality to His love. 'Sir', said Dr. Johnson to his
faithful Boswell, 'we form many friendships by mistake,
imagining people to be different from what they really
are'. But Jesus was not so deluded. Jesus's knowledge
of man gives potency to His sympathy. As God He knows
our frame and as man, since He was made in all things
like unto His brethren, He knows our need. If He had
partial knowledge He could not have perfect sympathy.
It is the fact of His knowledge which gives finality to
His authority. Whatever Jesus declared is not only the

right word it is also the final word. All else that is said to purpose is but a faint echo of His sayings. He speaks with final authority concerning God, and life and sin and redemption and judgement. And it is His knowledge which gives supremacy to His commands, victory to His purpose and urgency to His appeals.

Besides a knowledge that was unique there was also in Christ a power that was divine. We are not thinking here of His miracles. It is, as a matter of fact, a question whether these were performed by virtue of His being a perfect man under the Spirit or by virtue of His divine nature. We must, however, observe that His miracles were, as Erasmus remarked, acted parables. Jesus sought to bring all His miracles into the realm of the spiritual. In this sense they become eloquent sermons, preaching Christ's readiness to come to the remedy of all in need. Unlike the prophets of the Old Testament the miracles of Jesus were not an alien and occasional addition to His person and vocation. They were profoundly 'natural' to Jesus. It is thus important to observe that He did not need to entreat each of His miracles from God by prayer (cf. 1 Kings 17. 20f.; 2 Kings 4.3 3f.; Josh. 5. 16f.; Mark 6. 41; John 6. 11). His miracles were, so to speak, the forth-flashings of His total being. They were so much His own that His was a power He could communicate to others (Matt. 10. 8; Mark 6. 7 cf. Acts 3. 6; 9. 34, etc.). The miracles of Jesus were a service of love and grace; yet for all those who had hearts to understand they were of such a nature as to bear witness to Him as sent by the Father (John 5. 36). The miracles of Jesus are part of the fact of Jesus. They demonstrate the reality of blessings from the throne of God upon men and they proclaim the saving deeds of the gospel. They are of a pattern with the Person self-disclosed in the record. In a very definite manner they unveil His glory (John 2. 11; 11. 4).

Throughout the days of His ministry Jesus gave self-disclosures in such a fashion as to make the conclusion inescapable that He can be understood only in terms of Godhood. He forgives sins (Mark 2. 5-10; Luke 7. 48). Only one sinned against can forgive, and in the last analysis sin is against God (Ps. 51. 4). Who can forgive sins but God alone? asked the scribes with right insight, but wrong conclusion, when Jesus declared the paralytic man forgiven (Mark 2. 7). That the man was aware that he was forgiven is demonstrated by the fact that he arose and walked. Here was Jesus doing the works of Christ (Matt. 11. 2). He was disclosing Himself as the bearer of God's salvation, as the power of God for the deliverance of man. He is doing what God alone can do for man.

It may be marked also that Jesus showed Himself to be supreme over the temple (Matt. 12. 6), over the Sabbath (Matt. 12. 8), and over the kingdom of Satan (Matt. 12. 24f.).

Without going further into the evidence, we have enough before us to admit the conclusion that the self-manifestation of Jesus in what He knew Himself to be, and in what He declared Himself to be, and in what He showed Himself to be, demonstrate that He who stands behind everything in the Gospels is a divine Person, who came to fulfil a unique vocation. The teaching He gave, the deeds He wrought, the commands He gives, the authority He wields, the knowledge He possesses, the position in which He placed Himself, assume this fact about Jesus at every point. He is such a One we know God should be, and which we feel God would be in the sphere of human life and experience. When, therefore, they asked Him whether He were the Christ, the Son of God, the Son of the Blessed (Luke 22. 70; Mark 14. 61), He did not hesitate with the answer. He knew that He was; and He said so.

Further reading:
A. W. Argyle, *The Christ of the New Testament*, especially
ch. 2 (London, 1952).
G. Vos, *The Self-Disclosure of Jesus* (Grand Rapids, 1950).
L. Morris, *The Lord from Heaven* (London, 1958).
C. S. Lewis, 'The Shocking Alternative' *Mere Christianity*
(London 1952).

THE BIBLICAL ATTESTATION OF CHRIST AS TO HIS DEITY
(i) In the Preaching of the Church

One thing that strikes us as we read the fragments of
the primitive preaching and proclamation in the early
chapters of Acts is that it is all centred upon the Person
of Christ. The material which provides us with this
summary of early Christian Christology comprises
Peter's sermon at Pentecost (2. 14-40); his address to
the people in the temple (3. 12-26); his defence before
the council (4. 8-12); and his sermon at Caesarea
(10. 36-43). To this may be added the speech of Stephen
before the Sanhedrin (ch. 7), and Philip's conversation
with the Ethopian chancellor (8. 30-36).

These passages all reveal that there was from the first
a doctrine of Christ (cf. 5. 28). James Denney considers
the fact that from the beginning there was a Christology
important as showing how much off the mark are those
who have maintained that Jesus is not indispensable to
the gospel. The truth is rather the very reverse of this.
What is the prime emphasis in the proclamation of
these first preachers of the Christian message is, not so
much what Jesus taught, but who He is. It was because
of who He is, that they saw value, and meaning and
relevance in what He did.

Inevitably Peter started from the historical person;
with the One he knew and with whom he had kept
company. While on earth Jesus was among men as a
man approved by God by signs and miracles which He
did (2. 22). He was anointed by God with special

63

power (4. 27). This approval and this anointing declare Him to be both Lord and Christ (2. 36 cf. 10.36). The great declaration, Jesus Christ is Lord, may well be, as has been suggested, the earliest of Christian creeds.

His unique position is attested by His resurrection from the dead and exaltation to the right hand of the Father. The term 'Father' (2. 33) slips naturally from the lips of Peter who must have had in the background of his mind the disclosures in the Upper Room when Jesus spoke so intimately of 'my father'—'I and the Father are one'. It is the Jesus whom Peter had known and who is now vindicated as Lord and Christ, who communicates the power of the Holy Ghost (2. 33), heals (3. 16), and forgives (5. 31), and is ordained to be the Judge of all (10. 42). The ringing assurance of the primitive preaching is, then, Jesus Christ, He is Lord of all (10. 36).

The one place where the title Son of God occurs (8. 37) is shown by manuscript evidence not to be part of the original text. But if Jesus is not actually called Son of God in our present sources, He is presented in such terms as to put Him beyond explanation in human categories. He is seen as seated at the right hand of God, participating in the divine glory and sharing with God in the government of the world (5. 31; 10. 36, 42). His lordship is specially mentioned (2. 20, 25, 35; 4. 26; 10. 36 etc.). In view of the Septuagint use of the designation 'Kurios' (Lord) as a name for Jehovah, it is not easy to resist the conclusion that the application of it to Jesus could have suggested anything other to Jewish minds than that He possessed a super-human character (cf. 2. 25, 36 etc.). There is a strong assertion of His sinlessness (3. 14; 4. 27). He is the true Object of faith (3. 16; 10. 43) and the giver of salvation (3. 25; 4. 12; 5. 31).

As Christ He is the focus of all prophecy—to Him bear

all the prophets witness (3. 18; 10. 43; cf. 2. 25; 8.28f.).
As Christ He must suffer (3. 18). It is no matter of
surprise therefore to find Him referred to in the most
natural way as the Suffering Servant of Jehovah (3. 18,26;
4. 27, 30 RV), and as the Lamb for the slaughter of
Isaiah 53 (8. 32f). The whole content of the
primitive proclamation can be given its summary
in Peter's own words: Neither is there salvation in
any other, for there is none other name under heaven
given among men whereby we must be saved
(4. 12).

The conviction is steady throughout the material
before us that all the spiritual blessings which man can
possess and God bestow either here or hereafter are
because of this Christ who lived, died, rose again from the
dead and reigns as Lord. He stands on God's side con-
fronting men with the offer of God's salvation
(2. 38; 3. 18-20).

Jesus is not presented as the first Christian or as the
Founder of the Christian Religion. As the Lamb
brought to the slaughter and the Lord at the right hand
of God, as the Suffering Servant of Jehovah and the
Prince of Life, He is the sum total of all that Christianity
means. 'The apostles and their converts are not persons
who share the faith of Jesus; they are persons who
have Jesus as the Object of their faith, and who believe
in God through Him'.

The preaching of the Church is, therefore, anchored
in Jesus, but the anchor of the Church's faith is within
the veil, where the Jesus of history is the Christ of faith.

(ii) In the Teaching of the Apostles
  (a) The Petrine Epistles
In the Petrine speeches of Acts and First Peter there
is the same thought of Jesus being delivered to death by
the determinate counsel and foreknowledge of God

(Acts 2. 23; 4. 28; 10. 42; 1 Pet. 1. 2, 20). The prophecy from Psalm 118. 22 of Christ as the Stone set at nought of the builders is quoted (Acts 4. 11; 1 Pet. 2. 6). There is, perhaps, an advance in Peter's thought in the Epistle in that the article is dropped from the title Christ; it is now a proper name.

Although Peter does not use the term Son he has the correlative Father (1. 2), which indicates a unique relationship. The pre-existence of Christ is more clearly emphasised in the epistle. He was foreknown before the foundations of the world (1. 20); and that this cannot be explained in an ideal sense is made evident by the added declaration that He was manifested at the chosen time. He was foreknown because He was there to be known before.

He is the medium of spiritual worship (2. 5); the chief cornerstone (2. 6); the Bishop and Shepherd of souls (2. 25); and the chief Shepherd yet to be manifested (5. 4). In Him we are called to eternal glory (5. 10) and through Him God is glorified (4. 11); while the believing man is called to sanctify Him in his heart as Lord (3. 15 RV).

In I Peter the trinitarian formula is more clearly indicated (1. 2), and the deed of salvation is conceived of as implicating the Father, the Spirit and Jesus Christ; while in many passages it is difficult to say if the term God is applied to the Father or to Christ.

In this epistle Jesus Christ is proclaimed as the sinless Saviour whose sufferings are a pattern for the tried believer (2. 21, 22; 4. 1, 13; 5. 9), and the ground on which man is redeemed (1. 19; 2. 24; 3. 18). This last reference unites the person and work of Christ in the divine act of man's salvation. 'For Christ also died for sins once for all, the righteous for the unrighteous, that he might bring us to God' (RSV). He the righteous for us the unrighteous; here is the paradox of the cross. He dealt with sin 'once and for all'; here is the perfection of the cross. He died that He might bring us to God; here is the purpose of the cross (cf. 2. 23-25).

The key word in Peter's Second Letter is knowledge (cf. 1. 2, 3, 5, 6, 8, 16, 20 etc.). He stresses three great themes all centring on Christ: the Christian life has its source in Christ; Christian truth has its location in Christ; and Christian hope has its eye on Christ. By the act of faith believers have become sharers in the common salvation which is in the righteousness of God and our Saviour Jesus Christ. The name Jesus Christ is here unusually solemnly reinforced by the prefix Lord or Saviour or both. Allusion is made to the testimony given to the Sonship of Christ by God the Father at the transfiguration when the three disciples were eye-witnesses of His majesty (1. 16-18).

(b) The Johannine Epistles and Revelation

The three opening verses of John's First Epistle appear as an implicit commentary on the Prologue with which John opens his Gospel. The term Word (Logos) may well have given the impression to some of Christ as a sort of mystical figure. The Gospel had, of course, clearly insisted upon the human personality of the incarnate Word, but whatever doubt remained about the actuality of Christ, John here seeks to remove. And he does this by an appeal to personal testimony (1. 1). The presence of Christ among men had been audible, visible and tangible. To deny this is to make Christ a liar (4. 2, 3; 5. 5). Not only does John insist upon identifying Christ with the human Jesus (2. 22), but equally he insists upon relating this Jesus Christ to God (5. 5). So complete, indeed, is the identification that in such passages as 5. 10 and 5. 20 it is impossible to say to which the writer refers.

In two passages (3. 5 and 8), John brings the manifestation of Christ into relation to sin and the devil. He came to take away sin and to destroy the works of the devil. Christ is our propitiation (2. 2; 4. 10), our means of cleansing (1. 7) and our advocate (2. 1). In contrast, then, with the Fourth Gospel in which the theme is elaborated, Jesus is the Christ, we have in the epistles of John the theme, Christ is Jesus. What John states in his letter he presupposes in the two lesser ones: God meets us in Christ—and Christ is Jesus.

The title 'Lamb of God' is a recurring one in the Book of Revelation, being found some twenty-nine times. The word used for Lamb is not, however, the same as that which occurs in John's Gospel (1. 29, 36). The term used in the Apocalypse does, however, appear in the Gospel (21. 15), although it is not there applied to Christ. In I Peter He is likened to a lamb (1. 19). Revelation, as the Fourth Gospel and the Epistles of John, has the idea of Christ as the Word. He is the Word of God in Revelation (19. 13). In the First Epistle He is the Word of Life (1. 1). In the Gospel He is the Word absolutely (1. 1). The Epistles present Christ as the Life, and to have Him is to have eternal life (5. 11, 12. cf. 1. 2).

In the Revelation, however, the concern is not so much with Christ's Sonship in the past as with His redemption in the present and His Kingship in the future. The dominating conceptions are that of Redeemer and King. He is at once the Royal-Saviour.

His earthly life is consequently presupposed since it was in the days of His flesh that He wrought out redemption. There is therefore frequent reference to His life on earth as the sphere in which the redeeming act was performed and within which His kingly authority operates. Emphasized consequently is the humanity of the Christ, who in vision John sees moving amid the celestial sphere, with redemptive grace and in regal glory. He is of the tribe of Judah and the family of David

(5. 5; 22. 16). His death in Jerusalem is specifically mentioned (11. 8). We are given to feel right through that the One to whom such mystical terms as Lamb, Lion, the Word and the like are applied is none the less of our own nature (1. 13). Thus the book which exalts Jesus to the throne does not detach Him from the world. Throughout the whole unveiling of the exalted Christ, the historic Jesus breaks through, thereby showing the groundlessness of all theologies which fail to give to Him the unique significance of His appearance in history.

John, however, sees Christ in the super-sensuous world, above and beyond history and yet as the moving power of all things. Jesus therefore is set before us in the dual role of Redeemer within history and the Lord of all history. An examination of the passages where the phrase 'Lamb of God' occurs will reveal that it unites the two ideas of redemption and kingship. For the first connection such verses as 5. 9, 12; 7. 14; 12. 11; 22. 27 are significant. On the other side there is associated with the title the thought of sovereignty (5. 6, 8, 13; 6. 16; 7. 10; 22. 1, 3). The concepts of vicarious suffering and victorious love are here made one in the person of the redeeming and reigning Christ. At the very heart of God's sovereignty is sacrificial and suffering love.

Through the blood of Jesus salvation is made available to the believing heart which brings with it liberty (1. 5 RV), redemption (7. 14; 22. 14) and victory (12. 11). The Lamb has a place in the midst of the throne. His sovereignty relates to the churches (cf. 1. 11-18). Here Christ is presented as the Alpha and the Omega, the A and the Z; and all the colourful description of Him goes to accentuate His lordship. The most striking imagery is set before us to unveil His dignity and authority. Both the vision (1. 12-15a) and the voice (15b-18) of chapter one alike serve to reveal His sovereignty. He has the clothes of royalty, the head of glory, the eyes of brilliancy, the feet of victory, the voice of majesty and the hand of authority.

His sovereignty, too, relates to the world. The world-shaking movements which accompany the opening of the seals of the book are due to the 'wrath of the lamb' (6. 16); and His authority extends to the nations (12. 5). His sovereignty relates no less to the final victory of God. In the judgements of God He is the supreme Actor. It is He who comes with great power and glory to judge the world and save His people (17. 14-16; 22. 20). So the Morning Star shall arise and the Lamb shall be the light of the City Foursquare. For He is the Faithful Witness and the first-begotten from the dead and the Ruler of the kings of the earth (1. 5). He is King of kings and Lord of lords (17. 14; 19. 16).

Such a presentation of Christ places Him squarely on the side of the Godhead and must of necessity involve His essential deity. He is the object of divine honours. To Him both worship and praise are given in the same way as to God (5. 11, 12; 7. 10; 22. 8, 9). He is ministered to by saints as to God Himself (20. 6). He sits with God in His throne having the keys of Hades and death. He is the redeemer of men—and what it took a whole God to create cannot be redeemed by One reckoned to be only a half god. By applying to Him the words of Isaiah 44. 6, which in its Old Testament context describes the absolute eternity of Jehovah as the First and the Last, John gives to Jesus a position of equality with God. He belongs to the divine order of existence and as such can call God His Father in a special sense (1. 6; 2. 27; 3. 5; 14. 1). He is the One to whom the seven-fold perfection of God is ascribed (3. 1; 5. 6; cf. 1. 4; 4. 5). He possesses the secret of Jehovah and writes His mysterious Name upon the foreheads of

His saints (2. 17; 3. 12; 14. 1). In the final victory of God the kingdoms of this world are His in union with God, the God of Heaven, the Almighty (11.13 f.; cf. Matt. 4. 8-10).

(c) *The Epistle to the Hebrews*

The author of *Hebrews* has an array of terms in which he describes Jesus in His work: Pioneer, Apostle, Mediator, High Priest, Forerunner, Surety, Shepherd. But there is one term in which he seeks to open to us the inmost personality of Jesus and to unveil what He is in Himself. He is the Son of God, or more simply and absolutely 'the Son'. These other titles are descriptive of His office; that of 'the Son' is expressive of His essence. While these other terms reveal what He does, His relation to men, this has reference to what He is, His relation to God.

The Epistle to the Hebrews clearly expresses what must ever remain as the essential for Christian faith, the twofold significance of Christ. He is our Brother who inspires our love and confidence because He has made Himself one with us in our common lot and life. He is also apart from men and has the power to communicate new life and bring us near to God because He is separate from sinners and made higher than the heavens. But there is no speculative Christology in the Epistle, in the sense that no formal attempt is made to reconcile these two facts. Jesus is set forth as Son of God and as 'this man'. He is made less than the angels yet He is more than they.

The Sonship of Christ is the fundamental thing in this 'Word of Exhortation'. God hath spoken to us in One who is Son (en huiō)—in One, that is, who has the nature of Son. Westcott points out that the absence of the article in the Greek fixes attention upon His nature rather than upon His personality.

The Son is the appointed Heir to all things (1. 3). He reflects God's bright glory and is stamped with God's character and sustains the universe with God's own power. The word translated 'express image' (AV) is *charakter*, from which we derive our English word 'character'; and the word for 'person' is *hypostaseos* which has the idea of essence. Thus is the Son of God the very character of God's essential being: He has the stamp of God's character. Jesus is God thrown on the screen of human life. 'In Him all His Father shone, substantially expressed' (Milton).

As Son He has pre-eminence in the universe. He is the agent of creation and the channel of providence (1. 3, 10). To Him who can save, to create is but a small matter.

As Son He is pre-eminent to the angelic host. To no angel did God ever give the title Son. Christ could be made a little lower than the angels, because in eternity He was greatly above them.

The writer of the Hebrews is one with Paul in presenting Jesus as holding all things together, as the chain band of all existence, to use a phrase from Philo. To this writer as to the apostle to the Gentiles, creation is centred in Christ (Heb. 1. 2; Col. 1. 15f.). Thus Moses was but a servant in the house—but He is Son over the house. Three times in the epistle the term 'Heir' appears, and in each place the reference is to the Son's final glory as Redeemer. There is emphasized throughout the epistle the ascension and exaltation of the Son. The idea is usually pictured as the return of a priest from his sacrifice. In solemn procession He passes from the scene of sacrifice, conflict and victory up through the heavens, and in behind the veil, to the innermost sanctuary, and to the seat of power and authority at the right hand of the majesty on high. He enters heaven in the power of that blood, which is His indestructible life (7. 16), and there appears in the presence of God on our behalf, ever-living to make intercession for us. By His ascension, therefore, He is definitely marked out and installed as

Son of God with power (cf. Rom. 1. 4). As Son of God
He will come to judge and to reign (9. 27f.). To the
writer, Christ is accorded a place beside God. He is
more than the sinless angels. It was with Him God
conferred at the creation of the world. The Christology
of this epistle is the same 'higher Christology' that is
found in Paul and John. Chapter 1. 18 speaks of Him as
God, and 1. 10 as Lord. Thus must the writer have held
a view of Christ's person which made it natural for him
to apply to Him the titles 'God' and 'Lord'; titles with
which he was perfectly familiar as designations for the
supreme Deity.

(iii) The Pauline Christology

So much can be said about the Pauline Christology
that we find ourselves able to give the lines only along
which the subject can be followed. Two considerations,
however, must be kept well in mind as regards Paul's
understanding of the person in Christ. It must be
premised, first of all, that what the apostle has to say
respecting Him is in essential harmony with the primitive
Gospel. Paul did not introduce a strange Christ to the
theological world. He was not the originator of another
gospel, which is not another (Gal. 1. 6f.). What
we are saying here makes void the suggestion that it was
due to Paul that we have, among his other theological
accretions, the Son-of-God Christology. It was he, it is
held by some, who was the first to give to the title a
Christological connotation and thereby 'Paulinised'
the primitive gospel. The truth is rather that all Paul's
central conceptions, on grace, justification, salvation
through the blood of Christ, as well as his so-called
'higher Christology', came to him straight from the
heart of Jesus's message.

The other point to be made is that Paul's Christology
was, of course, coloured by the fact that his first en-

counter with Jesus was with Him as glorified Lord. It is here we have the dynamic centre of His understanding of Christ. Paul first found Christ on bended knee; and it was this glowing experience which is reflected in all his Christological statements. For the original disciples the astonishing thing was that Jesus, whom they knew and whose companions they were, and who had been put to death as a common criminal, should now be exalted to the very throne of God. To Paul the reverse was the astonishing wonder. He had been 'apprehended' by the living Lord on the Damascus road. The One who had so overwhelmed him by the sheer grace of God was declared to him to be the exalted Jesus (Acts 9. 5). He has now a place within the realm of Deity. How could this One take flesh and die? This is humility at its ultimate and its most Godlike (Phil. 2. 1f). For Paul the glory of Christ lay in the humilitation which brought Him within the human sphere to accomplish His divine work of salvation. For the other disciples the glory of Christ lay in His exaltation from the human sphere having died a death which was revealed to be on account of man's sin (cf. Acts. 2. 22, 33).

For Paul, it must be well marked, the Damascus road encounter was not the confirmation of a theory but the experience of a theophany. The notion that all the elements of Paul's Christology existed as floating ideas in Jewish messianism and oriental myths is out of harmony with the facts of the situation. Paul did not gather together all these speculations and on the Damascus road come to a reasoned conclusion by merely adding the name Christ to these apocalyptic fancies. Such a reading of Paul's conversion is, especially in the light of his later service in the gospel, as fantastic as it is eccentric. The truth is that here Paul found redemption through the very Jesus against whom he was fighting. He was in no mood to put that name at the head of any religious ideas. It was rather that this now exalted Jesus had put His name on Paul (cf. 1 Cor. 6. 11; 2 Cor. 4. 6; Gal. 1. 10; Gal. 1. 15, 16; etc., cf. Rom. 6. 16, 17, 20; 1 Cor. 7. 23; Eph. 6. 6 etc.). He was a 'debtor' who owed all he now possessed to Christ and who could only acknowledge his infinite debt by the full dedication of himself to Him who loved Him and gave Himself for Him. From that shining moment on the road outside Damascus Paul was Christ's servant; Christ's slave (doulos). Paul was the 'prisoner of Christ' for ever after, being led through the world in the triumphal train of the victorious Lord (2 Cor. 2. 14). He was now 'in Christ', living by the faith that is in the Son of God who had become One accursed for him that he might be declared righteous before God in a righteousness not his own.

Yet Paul's gospel—'my gospel' as he speaks of it (Rom. 2. 16; 2 Cor. 4. 3; cf. 1 Thess. 1. 5; 2 Thess. 2. 14; Gal. 2. 2) was not something learned at second-hand. It came to him directly by the revelation of Jesus Christ (Gal. 1. 16). Flesh and blood had not made it known to him; it had come from above (cf. Matt. 16. 17). He can consequently declare what he knew so personally and dynamically in his own experience: 'No man can say that Jesus is Lord except by the Holy Ghost' (1 Cor. 12. 3). Thus was Paul's gospel, Christ's gospel—the veritable Gospel of God (cf. Rom. 1. 1, 16; 15. 16, 19 etc.).

The transforming experience on the Damascus road brings into focus what was to be the heart of Paul's proclamation throughout the after years. Stabbed awake in his conscience by the appearance of Christ, Paul's first reaction was the question: 'Who art thou Lord?' The answer came 'I am Jesus whom thou art persecuting'.

Who art thou Lord? I am Jesus. There was the identity, the startling and staggering revelation. It was upon this fact that Paul was to lay emphasis. Jesus, He is Son of God (Acts. 9. 20), and very Christ (Acts 9. 22).

The centre of his gospel is, as he tells the Corinthians, the proclamation of 'Christ Jesus as Lord' (2 Cor. 4. 5).

Although Paul could assert that his gospel was no borrowed creed, that what he discovered of Christ came not by tradition from those who as apostles were 'in Christ' before him, yet all that he has to say about Christ is at one with the primitive faith. Paul was in no sense the 'second founder of Christianity'. He was not the second after Christ but one among those who were 'in Christ'. It is after all the same Spirit of God who is over all God's purposes of grace for mankind. Paul's emphasis upon the lordship of Christ is in harmony with all that his predecessors in the faith knew of Him. From the beginning Christ was seen as occupying the throne of the universe. He is the cosmic Redeemer and Lord whose universal sway is attested by the fact that God raised Him from the dead, to inaugurate an eternal kingdom. In Paul, as in the earliest sources of the New Testament, Christ's resurrection and exaltation are united with the reality of His lordship. It is those who confess that Jesus is Lord and believe in their hearts that God hath raised Him from the dead, who are the saved (Rom. 10. 9; cf. Rom. 8. 34; Eph. 1. 19-20 Col. 3. 1).

Paul's theology was therefore essentially the theology of the man in Christ; one redeemed by the action of the glorified Lord. From the risen Son of God flowed all the redeeming influences and from Him stemmed all the moral power requisite for the transformation of man into the image of Christ, the perfect Man.

This lordship of the exalted Christ is all-embracing. Over Jew and Greek, rich and poor, He is the same Lord to all that call upon Him. To this lordship all will be subject.

The lordship of Christ is the decisive factor within

the Church. The Church is His (cf. Matt. 16. 18; Rom. 16. 16 etc.), as it is God's (I Cor. 1. 2; 11. 22; 15. 9 etc.). Here is a relationship which does not detract from God but which rather exalts Christ to the status of deity. It is from this conviction of the absolute right of Christ as Lord within His Church that all the ethical demands of the New Testament are derived. The believer is related to Christ as slave to Master, and his highest ideal is to be made 'captive to obey Christ' (2 Cor. 10. 5). While the inner power controlling all his motives is the overmastering love of Christ who loved him even when he was yet a sinner (cf. 2 Cor. 5. 14: Rom. 5. 8). As bought with a price he must glorify the Lord who bought him. Christ is therefore 'the head of His body, the Church, and the fulness of Him who filleth all in all' (Eph. 1. 22).

His lordship extends to the universe and beyond (Eph. 1. 21). He is, to use Lightfoot's paraphrase of Col. 1. 15f, 'the perfect image, the visible representation of the unseen God. He is the Firstborn, the absolute Heir of the Father, begotten before the ages; the Lord of the universe by virtue of primogeniture and by virtue also of creative agency. For in Him and through Him the whole world was created, things in heaven and things in earth, things visible to the outward eye, and things cognizable to the outward perception. His supremacy is absolute and universal. All powers in heaven and earth are subject to Him. This subjection extends even to the most exalted and most potent of angelic beings, whether they be called Thrones or Dominions or Princedoms or Powers or whatever title of dignity man may confer upon them. Yes, He is first and He is last. Through Him, as the mediatorial Word, the universe has been created; and unto Him, as the final goal, it is tending. In Him is no before or after. He is pre-existent and self-existent before all worlds. And in Him as the binding and sustaining power, universal nature coheres and consists'.

As exalted Lord He is not however afar off and unheeding. He is ever-present within His Church, indwelling the hearts of His redeemed. He is the never-failing Guide, Comforter, and Leader of His people. Closer is He than breathing, nearer than hands and feet. To Him prayer is to be made in the fullest confidence that He is able royally and richly to answer (cf. John 14. 13, 14). Paul besought the Lord thrice, and it is clear that the 'Lord' he besought is the Christ he had come to know (cf. 2 Cor. 12. 2-10; cf. verse 9). To call upon the name of the Lord Jesus Christ was virtually a synonym for Christians. While to do anything for His sake was the true norm of service to God (cf. Acts 9. 16; Rom. 15. 30; 2 Cor. 12. 10; 3 John 7). By the application of the term Lord (*kurios*), the uniqueness of Christ as standing in the place of the Jehovah of the Old Testament is made manifest (cf. Rom. 10. 13; cf. Joel 2. 32). For Paul, indeed, the title Lord has a lofty significance. It has ceased in fact to be a title and has become the sacred expression of a personal devotion into which went the gratitude, love and loyalty of his redeemed being.

In two passages, Rom. 5. 12-21 and 1 Cor. 15. 44-49, Paul refers to Christ as the Second Adam. The title suggests the idea of Him as the Founder of a new humanity. In Him, as Representative, a new, that is, a redeemed humanity, takes its rise. The first Adam began a natural history, by him came death; he is a creature and perishable. The Second Adam stands at the head of a new humanity; by Him is resurrection. He is of heaven. The contrast between the first Adam, as a living soul, and the last Adam, as a quickening Spirit, brings out the fact that as such Christ is not merely within the natural order. He is a Being above nature by reason of the fact that in Him is life. He has life of

Himself and is capable of communicating it to those who are united to Him by faith. The new principle of life which is His to give is the forthflowing of that Spirit of holiness which is the inmost reality of His being.

This reference to the last Adam as a quickening Spirit raises the question of the relation between the exalted Christ and the Spirit. This however is a subject we cannot deal with here at any length except to say that while Paul does link the Spirit closely with the person of Christ as the redeeming activity of God in Christ within the human heart, the relation is not one of absolute identity. As the trinitarian passages must make clear (cf. Matt. 28. 19; 2 Cor. 13. 14; 1 Pet. 1. 2; Jude 20, 21), the relation is that of vital unity (cf. Gal. 2. 17; 1 Cor. 6. 11; 2 Cor. 4. 14 and Rom. 8. 11; 1 Cor. 12. 3 and 2 Cor. 3. 17 etc.).

Paul never uses the term Son of God except with a profound sense of reverence and devotion. It was not his view that Christ's is an acquired or attained Sonship. Such passages as Rom. 8. 32 and Col. 1. 13 cannot be taken to mean that He is Son because loved, but quite the reverse. He is loved because He is Son. It is as Son He came into the world. The suggestion that Paul initiated the 'Son of God Christology' can then have no substance from the one passage adduced for it, namely Romans 1. 4. Certainly Paul does here bring the Sonship of Christ into conjunction with the resurrection. Christ is described as coming of David's line according to the flesh and declared to be the Son of God in power according to the Spirit of holiness by the resurrection from the dead. Does this mean that the Pauline Christ is designated Son of God only after the resurrection? Of course it does not. No such adoptionist Christology can be deduced from this verse; and in any case such an understanding of Christ would be contrary to the whole tenor of the apostle's teaching. The word in the

79

original (horizō), signifies that although Christ was Son of God before the resurrection, yet He was openly appointed ('declared' AV) such among men by this transcendent and crowning event. 'The divine state', comments Godet, 'which followed the resurrection is a recognized not an acquired state.'

For all his emphasis, however, upon Christ as exalted Lord, as Cosmic Agent, and as Son of God, Paul was not altogether indifferent to the historic reality of the human Jesus. True, he never makes mention of His miracles, His prayerfulness, His faith, His habits among men. At the same time the view that Paul was so pre-occupied with the exalted Christ that he virtually turned Christianity from being a historic faith into a mere Christ-mysticism has little foundation in fact. It is not true that the Epistle to the Hebrews was written as a corrective to Paul; as an attempt to make secure again the Jesus of history.

The verse 2 Cor. 5. 16 has been urged as a warrant for the assumption that Paul did not bother himself with the Synoptic figure of Jesus. But the meaning here is not that Paul had no concern for the historic facts of Christ's life, but with the important truth that spiritual things must be spiritually interpreted. To know Christ in a fleshly way is not to have a real spiritual understanding of Him. Whether Paul did actually know Christ during the period of His humanity is uncertain, although it does seem likely. It would appear that he is suggesting in this passage that he did formerly know Him during the days of His flesh in an outward manner, but that now, in contrast, he knows Him in a living fellowship.

From the record of his sermons in Acts there are evidences of Paul's knowledge of the historical facts of the life of Jesus. He was probably well aware from his pre-Christian days of the kind of apologetic for Christ of which Stephen's speech was an example. After his conversion Paul was baptised and certainly not without some knowledge of the Christ whose name he had taken upon him. He must have become acquainted with some of the facts about Jesus during the three years in Arabia. He went up to Jerusalem on a special fifteen days mission according to Galatians 1. 18, and there he talked with Peter. He went up to interview Peter—'to history' (historēsai) him; only, of course, that is not good English. Paul worked for long periods in company with Barnabas, John Mark, Silas, Luke, all of whom were certainly in possession of the facts of the life and teaching of his Lord. It is incredible to suggest that he would not have learned from them something of these matters, or that he was not interested in what the Lord in whom he gloried said and did. For Paul the fact is rather that he regarded a saying of Jesus as the highest authority he can quote. Only when he has no commandment as such from the Lord does he admit his own commandment, though he believes himself to be inspired of the Spirit (cf. 1 Cor. 7. 10, 12, 25, 40; 9. 14).

A study of the Epistles of Paul reveals his knowledge of the historic Jesus. There is much obviously presupposed for he was writing from faith to faith and for faith's understanding. His epistles are not missionary propaganda; they are for the churches who were in possession of the historic facts. There are, however, impressive passages in which he refers to Christ's entry into human history. He was 'made of a woman, made under the law' (Gal. 4. 4). He set an example of courage under persecution (Rom. 15. 2f). He instituted the Last Supper, was killed upon the Cross. Of His character outlined in the factual story of His life, Paul has much to say. The glory of the believer is to be conformed into the image of Christ; to express, for example, 'the meekness and gentleness of Christ' (2 Cor. 10. 1). 1 Corinthians 13 is nothing if it is not a portrait of the

Saviour. Paul not only quotes the authority of Christ but records the unwritten saying of His: 'Remember the words of the Lord Jesus how He said it was more blessed to give than to receive' (Acts. 20. 35). Such injunctions as 'Judge not that ye be not judged'; 'Be careful for nothing' and the like are more than an echo of our Lord's teaching.

For Paul, then, it is a real Jesus who is Lord. And He is Lord for Paul in the very highest and holiest sense. For, as we have seen Paul applies to Him without hesitation the term Lord (Kurios) which the Septuagint uses to translate the Hebrew 'Jehovah' (cf. 1. Cor. 1. 31; 2 Cor. 3. 16; 10. 17; Eph. 4. 8; 2 Thess. 1. 9). Furthermore, the Old Testament 'day of the Lord' or 'day of Jehovah' became for Paul, without any awareness that he is doing violence to truth, 'the day of Christ' (cf. Amos 5. 18; Joel 2. 1; 1 Thess. 5. 2; cf. 1 Cor. 5. 5; Phil. 1. 6; 2 Thess. 1. 9). There is, therefore, no doubt in Paul's mind as to the true status of Christ. He is essentially Divine—fully within the area of Deity. Equally with God, He is the source of all spiritual blessings for the people of God (Rom. 1. 5, 7; 1 Cor. 1. 3; 2 Cor. 1. 2; Gal. 1. 3). He does for us what God does and is for us what God is (cf. 1 Cor. 15. 10; 2 Cor. 17. 9; 1 Cor. 13. 29; 2 Cor. 12. 8; 2 Thess. 3. 5; 1 Cor. 1. 8; Rom. 4. 4; Gal. 1. 16; 2 Cor. 5. 18; 10. 8; 13. 10; Phil. 3. 12; 1 Cor. 16. 23; 2 Cor. 12. 8; Phil. 2. 5-11).

He is consequently for Paul the 'image' (eikon) of the invisible God (Col. 1. 15). He is the One in whom God is seen absolutely. For in Him the very fulness of God took up its permanent abode in bodily form (Col. 2. 9). While originally in the fullest possession of Godhead yet He did not maintain this exclusive state as a prize to be held to, but took to Himself the form of a man and in that state lived a life of obedience even unto the death of the cross (Phil. 2. 7, 8). Does Paul then hesitate to apply to

82

Him the appellation God in the very fullest sense? He has made Him so Godlike that He cannot be less than God. There are, as we have noted, passages in which God and Christ are brought into the most intimate conjunction. In 2 Thessalonians 1. 12, the statement 'the grace of our God and Lord Jesus Christ' seems to make the identity definite and thus to assert Christ's absolute Deity. Titus 2. 13 (cf. verse 10), assuming its Paulinity, most certainly makes Jesus Christ our great God and Saviour. True to Paul's Christology is therefore his doxology of Romans 9. 5. It is a much debated question whether the words 'God over all blessed for ever' are to be taken as a further description of Christ or as a separate doxology referring to the Almighty. The structure of the sentence favours the first. It is on dogmatic grounds only that some have refused to allow that Paul is here making an unequivocal assertion of Christ's essential Deity. The suggestion that such a declaration must be regarded as 'too advanced' for him begs the question. It is our view that God has revealed Himself fully within the area of the 'closed canon' of Scripture and that, therefore, the Christ designated 'very God of very God' and of 'the same substance with the Father' of the later creeds, is the declared Christ of the New Testament. It cannot be reckoned as outside the faith and the proclamation of Paul, therefore, to make this full and final confession of Christ. The words of Romans 9. 5 may, then, be taken to read 'Christ... over all God blessed for ever', and thus, as H. R. Mackintosh says, they are 'an explicit assertion of Christ's deity'. Such an assertion is only the natural and legitimate climax of Paul's Christology, as we have seen the outlines of it in what has gone before.

Confession is made throughout of God the Father (e.g. Rom. 8. 15) and of the Lord Jesus (10. 9). The two are not confused; yet they are intimately related. We are thus led on naturally to the great trinitarian passages of the Pauline letters, in which the work of the Father, Son and Spirit is unfolded in relation to man's redemption. God is known as Father, through the Son by the Spirit (cf. e.g. Eph. 1. 3-14; 2. 18, 22). The 'Trinitarian form of experience' with the trinitarian benediction of 2 Corinthians 13. 14, however, make no less sure the unity of the Christian experience of God. It is God who is known as the Divine Father, through Him who is Divine Son and in Him who is Divine Spirit. This is both the authentic voice of Revelation as it is the living reality of experience. When, therefore, we confess Christ's Deity we simply give Him His right name. In truth the whole New Testament Christology is but the unfolding of the proclamation made at His birth: 'of Mary was born Jesus, who is called Christ' (Matt. 1. 16). He is the anointed One. His name is to be called Jesus, for He shall save His people from their sins (Matt. 1. 21). He is the atoning One. And they shall call His name Emmanuel, which being interpreted is, *God* with us (Matt. 1. 23). He is the abiding One.

Further reading:
P. Gardener-Smith, *The Christ of the Gospels* (Cambridge, 1938).
E. M. Sidebottom, *The Christ of the Fourth Gospel* (London, 1961).
J. P. Alexander, *A Priest Forever* (London, 1937).
E. Andrews, *The Meaning of Christ for Paul* (New York, 1949).
James S. Stewart, *A Man in Christ* (London, 1938).

Chapter Five

THE TITLES THAT ARE REVEALING

THE PRE-EXISTENT ONE

Although the actual title The Pre-existent One is not applied to Jesus in the New Testament, all the data for His pre-existence are there. The application of the category of pre-existence to Him was not a mere deduction of faith on the part of the first disciples. It is not our view of the facts that the biblical statements regarding Christ were the result of human musings on the Christ-fact. The truth is rather that the apostles were guided by the Spirit of God in making their profound declarations respecting the Saviour whom they had come to know. This fact means, however, that in making their statements regarding the pre-existence of Christ the divinely instructed apostles were not going beyond what was already implicit in Christian faith as already proclaimed and experienced.

One aspect of the Kingship of the Messianic Figure of the Old Testament was his close association or even identity with the personal revelation of Jehovah (cf. Isa. 9. 6). In the prophetic utterance of Micah (5. 2), the Messiah who comes forth as Ruler from Bethlehem is, at the same time, one 'whose goings forth are of old, from ancient days'.

In what may be called the more popular teaching of Christ as recorded in the Synoptic Gospels, His continued existence to the end of time is clearly stated. But there are passages in which His pre-existence is either specifically indicated or definitely implied. The title Son of Man, as we have seen, and Son of God, as we shall see, certainly carry the idea that Bethlehem did not begin the account of His existence. He is the One who was to come (Matt. 11. 3)—the sent One (Mark 12. 6; cf. Luke 7. 19; Matt. 21. 9; 23. 39; John 6. 14; 11. 27). The question Christ asked the Pharisees concerning the Messiah's relationship to David suggests that in the background of Jesus's mind was the realization of His pre-existence before His birth of the seed of David (Matt. 22. 41-45; Mark 12. 35-37; Luke 20. 41-44).

By His complete silence regarding His human birth and by His seeming refusal to admit enduring ties with His earthly family Jesus may well have intended to force upon enquiring minds the question, From whence then is He? (Mark 3. 31f; Luke 2. 48f; cf. Mark 6. 3; John 8. 41). And the famous declaration of Matthew 11. 27 can hardly have meaning if it be concluded that the existence of Christ, as Son of God, took its start within the framework of human history. The knowledge that Jesus claimed is of such a nature that it could not have been acquired by a created being within the limits of a life as brief as that of Jesus. A knowledge so intimate of God's inner nature and hidden counsels, which Jesus regarded Himself as possessing, must run beyond the bounds of history and the limits of time to be given adequate explanation. He was the Son of God 'with a prologue of eternal history and an epilogue of the same'. Jesus is not simply throned upon the world's history only, He is and He always was, the Son of God's love—the everlasting Son of the Father, throned at God's right hand, as the Key to all history; and its Judge.

References to His pre-existence, it is sometimes objected, are scarce and oblique in the Synoptics for the reason that the idea had no secure place in Christ's own consciousness. Such 'concordance criticism', as P. T. Forsyth speaks of it, is not so serious as is seemingly supposed. Is it not rather more legitimate to suggest that the references are few just because the awareness of His pre-existent glory held such a large place in the thought of Jesus? Deep things are not usually paraded; the captain is not loquacious in the rapids, nor does he talk seamanship in the storm. It was not Jesus's usual habit to satisfy idle curiosity. He would leave the truth about Himself to be given from above; to be discovered and appreciated through faith in and fellowship with Himself. It was, therefore, His custom to charge those He healed and cleansed to keep silence and not to make Him known.

When, however, we turn to John's Gospel, where the audience is not so much the general public as His disciples, the idea of pre-existence is expressly stated. Jesus Himself declares such a unique relationship—a veritable substantial identity indeed between Himself and the Father—which did not begin with His becoming flesh (3. 3; 6. 33-42). He co-existed with the Father prior to the days of Abraham (8. 58), and before ever the earth was (17. 5, 24). He descended from above (3. 21, 31) because He was 'from above' (8. 23). The conviction of His pre-existence is elsewhere maintained throughout the Gospel. The prologue clearly specifies it. He was there as the personal Word when the world was uttered into being and before His coming to be in flesh (1. 1-18). All through the record He is placed on the side of Deity and to such a One the declaration of pre-existence is natural and necessary. No man hath seen God at any time, the Only Begotten Son who is in the bosom of the Father, he hath declared Him (1. 18). This faith of the writer's in Christ's eternal existence is shared by John the Baptist (1. 30). So surely stated throughout is the Son's equality of nature with the Father that the whole Gospel depicts Him as sharing a community of life with the Father before the ages. There is no thought of His Sonship beginning within time—there is no adoptionist, no achievement Christology here.

Every one of Paul's epistles takes Christ's pre-existence for granted. In some passages, however, it is specially stated as having soteriological and ethical power and purpose (2 Cor. 8. 9; Phil. 2. 5f). There are passages where Paul has what has been referred to as 'a Logos Christology without the term'. In Colossians 1. 15-20, for example, He is brought into relation with the created universe. Not priority only, but *eternal* priority to all creation, is asciibed to him. He *is*, with the 'is' of an eternal present, before all time (Col. 1. 17). The passage teaches the supreme royalty of Jesus Christ. He upon whom all creation depends is outside the created. In His pre-incarnate state He is the Prior of all creatures, and the Agent of their coming into existence. Thus He possesses a supremacy, eternal, absolute and universal (Col. 1. 15, 16; cf. Eph. 1. 10, 14).

The passage Philippians 2. 5-7 has been described as 'the amplest and most deliberate of all St. Paul's declarations on the theme'. There are perhaps few statements in Scripture which have occasioned more comments than this. Leaving these out of account, however, the one fact upon which there is fairly general agreement is that here the apostle sets forth in the plainest terms the doctrine of Christ's pre-existence. He who dwelt within the infinite glory took a human life and went to the depths of humiliation. The contrast between what He was and what He chose to become is immense. The importance of the statement is highlighted when it is remembered that Paul was not intending a formal doctrinal declaration of Christ's prior existence. It comes in almost incidentally, in the midst of what is virtually 'an ethical sermon'. Paul would illustrate the vast love He disclosed in descending to our level and below, so that believers might be like-minded and take the way of humility. By thus incidentally, as it were, referring to the glory which was His before His coming within our human ways, Paul is making evident that the truth was well known to those of the Christian Way. It was part and parcel of the gospel he had preached unto them.

Apart from these two important passages there are other statements which must also be taken to allude to our Lord's pre-existence. 2 Corinthians 8. 9, for example, draws a contrast between the riches He surrendered when He temporally abdicated the throne and the poverty He assumed when He entered our human conditions. Verses such as Romans 8. 3, 1 Corinthians 10. 4, and Galatians 4. 4 have, too, certain reference to the actual and personal existing of the Son of God before His appearance on the stage of the world's history.

It is not possible to explain away such statements by saying that they mean no more than that He existed merely as an idea in the mind of God; that He existed, that is, in the divine foreknowledge only, but not as a divine actuality. No such exegesis can suit the passages themselves nor do justice to the whole New Testament understanding of the Son of God who came to be the Redeemer of man. Equally impossible is the suggestion that Paul was merely taking up into his account of Christ Jewish notions of the ideal 'pre-existence of their Great Sanctities'. True enough, the Jews did speak of the ideal existence of their Law and their Temple, but they had not, and could not, have cherished the idea of an actual personal pre-existent Messiah. Nor can it be maintained that the thought of pre-existence came to Paul through the Philonic theory of an ideal or heavenly man,

named by Philo, 'the First Man'. Paul's reference in
1 Corinthians 15. 44-49 is to 'the Second Man'; while
the context of the passage shows that it is the exalted
Christ not the pre-existence of Christ which is here in
view.

The idea of our Lord's pre-existence is not wanting
for support outside the definite statements of John's
Gospel and the Pauline writings. It is presented clearly
in other New Testament productions. The opening verses
of the Epistle to the Hebrews implies that the Sonship
of Christ goes back beyond the time of His partaking of
flesh and blood. He existed as having His origin in God
and as God before time was, and before His work of
atonement on earth and His ministry in heaven. From
what we have seen of the Christology of Revelation
Christ's pre-existence has there the strongest support.
Further reading:
P. T. Forsyth, *The Person and Place of Jesus Christ*, ch. 10
   (London, 1909).
V. Taylor, *The Name of Jesus*, (London, 1959).

THE SON OF GOD

Only on a few occasions does Jesus designate Himself
Son of God in the Synoptic Gospels. Thirty-two times,
however, is He called such by others, Himself sometimes
adopting the title or accepting it in a manner as appropriate to Himself. But He often spoke of God as His
Father with a force which reveals a sense of profound
and unique relationship to God. There are several
instances of His use of the term 'Son', often with the
prefix to underscore His special sense of union with
God His Father—'the Son', 'His Son', 'my Son', 'My
Beloved Son' and the like. Apart from these particular
references, in some of the Parables the title is implied.
In the parable of the Vineyard the 'beloved son' who is
'the heir' cast out and killed is clearly a reference to
Jesus Himself (Matt. 21. 38). Less clear, perhaps, is

the implication of Jesus's Sonship in the parable of the Marriage Feast (Matt. 22. 2f). Deeper, however, than the mere mathematical occurrences of the titles relating to His Sonship is the basic fact that His work for men is made to rest throughout the whole New Testament upon the special and personal relation between Him as Son, and God as Father. Thus, when applied to Jesus even in the Synoptics the title is meant to convey the existence of a deep kinship between God and Christ.

The term Son of God was, of course, well known in Jewish circles. In the Old Testament it is applied to angels (Job 38. 7; cf. 1. 6; 2. 1), to magistrates (Ps. 82. 6, 7); to the Hebrew nation (cf. Exod. 4. 22f.), to the Theocratic King (cf. 2 Sam. 7. 17; Ps. 89. 27). In the New Testament it is referred to the first man (Luke 3. 38), and to believers (cf. John 1. 12; 1 John 3. 1).

All these examples, however, show that the under-girding idea is that of a special nearness to God; of special privileges and endowments conferred by Him. In the reference to Jewish kings we have more probably the source of the title as referred to Christ. The application of the title to the nation culminated in that of the kings; while in its turn the application of it to the kings found its fulfilment in Him who summed up in Himself the regal idea in Israel. Basic, however, as is this politico-messianic idea, it does not give the ultimate sense of the term as applied to Christ. All the passages in the Synoptics and John's Gospel point rather to the personal qualities of Him who bears the title and to a unique relationship to God whose Son He is said to be. The official or messianic sense of the term describes not essential nature but office. As Heir and Representative of God, the Messiah could truly bear the title Son of God without reflection on His nature. Yet although the term has a messianic flavour, it is not as a synonym for Messiah that the term Son of God is used in the

Gospels and the New Testament generally. When demoniacs applied it to Jesus it may well be in a messianic sense, and the same may be true of the trial passage before the high priest (Matt. 26. 63; cf. verse 68). But in those passages where Jesus speaks of Himself as 'the Son' and calls God 'His Father', the official messianic idea is entirely absent. He is not, that is to say, called Son of God because He is Messiah; He is Messiah because He is Son of God.

Even explanations in terms of an ethical relationship between Jesus and God are not sufficient to exhaust the full significance of the designation Son of God. Passages such as 'O my Father if it be possible . . .' (Matt. 26. 39) and 'Father into Thy hands . . .' (Luke 23. 46) may be taken as expressive of this personal ethical relationship. And the profound words of Matthew 11. 27 may be read as the climax of this ethico-religious sentiment. These Johannine-like words are not however a passing emotion in the self-consciousness of Jesus; they are the outflow of a settled conviction and a habitual mood. There is a relationship pre-supposed which is one of absolute intimacy.

The ethical relationship demands a deeper and profounder one. Thus the title Son of God is no official designation of office or no pattern sonship for discipleship, for He never became a Son. Jesus unfailingly spoke of God as 'my Father' and 'your Father' but never as 'our Father'. To say, with Harnack, that the name Son means nothing but the knowledge of God, is far from the truth. For the mind of Jesus the unclouded consciousness of an eternally unshared Sonship is the supreme reality. The ethical union implies a metaphysical one—a union of nature. Christ spoke of God as Father and Himself as Son with a 'naturalness' which indicated His moral perfection. Thus to say that Jesus was in ethical relation to God is to say that He was in essential relation to Him. The consciousness of His own sinlessness gives Him the right to use the title without strain or stain, and thus to set Him apart from others. Between Jesus and God, indeed, all things are common. It is the filial consciousness not the messianic consciousness which is the basic fact of our Christian faith and gospel.

In John's Gospel the presentation of the Sonship of Christ has a larger place than in the Synoptics. But the essential facts are still the same. Here we find Jesus calling for faith in Himself as the Son of God (John 10. 35), and manifestly accepting the declaration of it (cf. 11. 27). It was for the purpose of establishing this faith in Him as Son of God that the Gospel itself was written (20. 31).

A new thought however is the description of the Son as 'only begotten'. The word used in 1. 14, 18; 3. 16, 18 (cf. 1 John 4. 9) for 'only begotten'—monogenes—underlines the fact that His Sonship is unique. According to Westcott the thought is centred in the personal Being of the Son and not in His generation. Christ is the One only Son, the One to whom the title belongs in a sense completely special and which distinguishes Him from the many children of God (cf. 1. 12f.). In contrast with others He is *Only* Son; the Son that never was, is, or shall be other than Son. In the Septuagint the word 'monogenes' is used to translate the Hebrew word for 'only' (jachid, cf. Judg. 11. 34); and the only begotten one is the only beloved one (cf. Gen. 22. 2, 12, 16— where the Septuagint has 'agapētos', 'beloved', for 'only'; cf. Mark 12. 6).

In his epistles John speaks of the Son with the same doctrinal overtones. As Son He was sent by the Father (1 John 4. 9, 10, 14), and to Him the Father bears witness (1 John 5. 9f). He is the true object of faith (1 John 5. 5, 10, 13) whose blood cleanses from sin

(1 John 1. 7). He is manifested to undo the works of the devil (1 John 3. 8; cf. 3. 5), and as such must be confessed (1 John 4. 15) or denied (1 John 2. 23). With the Father He bestows grace, mercy and peace (2 John 3).

The Pauline epistles and the Epistle to the Hebrews use, as we have observed, the title 'Son' or 'Son of God' in such a way as to make clear that they regarded Him as being perfectly at one and at home with God in His ultimate nature.

Further reading:
G. Vos, *The Self-Disclosure of Jesus*, chs. 10, 11, 12.
J. Jeremias, *Abba*, (Göttingen, 1966).
J. Jeremias, *The Central Message of the New Testament* (London, 1965).

We have drawn attention to the fact that the only begotten One is the Beloved One. In such passages as Matthew 3. 17, Mark 1. 11, and Matthew 17. 5 the 'Agapētos' would appear to be a separate title. Christ is to the Father 'The Beloved'. The designation was a current messianic one which united the two Old Testament statements of Psalm 2. 7, 'Thou art my Son, this day have I begotten thee', and Isaiah 42. 1, 'Behold my Servant, whom I uphold; mine elect in whom my soul delighteth'. The title 'The Beloved' in its turn appears practically synonymous with the 'Chosen' or 'Elect' One of Jehovah (cf. Matt. 12. 18; Luke 23. 35). Paul in Colossians 1. 13 speaks of the kingdom of God's Beloved Son, or, the Son of His love. In so describing Him the apostle is simply reinforcing the special and unique relationship between God and Christ.

Further reading:
J. Armitage Robinson, *Note on 'Beloved' in St. Paul's Epistle to the Ephesians*, pp. 229-233 (London, 1903).

THE WORD OF GOD

The conception of Christ as the 'Logos' or the Word

of God, is a peculiarity of the Fourth Gospel (1. 1-18).
But it is implied in some measure in other parts of the
New Testament (cf. Col. 1. 15-18; Heb. 1. 2-4; Rev.
9. 13). The Old Testament has certain significant
statements in which the 'Word' is regarded as creative
action in the soul (Ps. 33. 6) and in the universe as a
whole (Prov. 8. 22f RV). The term occurs also frequently
in the works of the Jewish-Alexandrian philosopher,
Philo, a younger contemporary of John's. Scholars
debate whether the apostle was influenced in any
measure or to what extent in his teaching by Logos-
ideas which may well have been 'in the air'. This is a
question which need not concern us here, for the genesis
of the Logos doctrine is far less important than its
exodus. Of one fact, however, we are sure: the Prologue
is an integral part of the Gospel, and although the term
does not find a place in the body of the writing its
contents appear everywhere. More particularly does
the special significance of the Logos doctrine reappear
under the categories of Truth, Light and Life, which are
recurring themes throughout. The designation Truth
describes the Logos in its nature. The connotation
of the term is 'reality', and for the apostle, it is only in
the person of Christ the incarnate Logos that men can
take hold of the Divine reality.

The word 'Light' may be said to describe the Logos
in its source. Light is the immemorial symbol of all that
is divine and holy. Thus He has come as a Light into
the world; come from Him who is Light Unapproach-
able—except through Him.

The designation 'Life' describes the Logos in its
action. As Christ, the incarnate Word, He communicates
to those who receive Him, who believe in Him, eternal
life. This is the 'real' life, because it possesses a divine
quality.

The Fourth Gospel opens by presenting to us the

Logos in a threefold relationship. First, to Deity (1. 1). In the briefest possible way John emphasises the eternity of the Word—'in the beginning was the Word'. John does not say that the Word had a beginning. But he is asserting that when there came to be a beginning the Word was there. The existence of the Word is thus carried necessarily beyond the limits of time. Also made clear here is the separate personality of the Word—'and the Word was with God', or literally, 'towards' (pros) God, in, so to imply, the bond of an unclouded fellowship. Stressed also by John is the Deity of the Word— 'and the Word was God'. By no stretch can the term God which occurs here be given a different connotation from its use immediately before. The Word is not 'a' 'god' (with an indefinite article and a small g) in contrast with 'the' 'God' (with the definite article and a capital G). The Arians and their modern successors the Jehovah Witnesses get no support for their created deity, their honorary god, here.

This verse is at the basis of the whole Gospel. In itself it precludes the false notion that the Word became personal, either at the time of the creation or the Incarnation. The absolute eternal imminent relations of the Persons of the Godhead furnish the basis for the revelation which is declared to be made in Christ. Precisely because the Word was personally distinct from God, and is yet essentially God, He could make God known—for, to repeat, only through God is God known. Westcott notes how the three great clauses in which the essential nature of the Word is declared are brought into relation to time, mode of being, and character, and answer to the three great movements of the Incarnation of the Word in verse 14 of chapter one. 'He who was God'—'became flesh'. 'He who was with God'—'dwelt among us', 'He who was in the beginning'—'became' 'came to be' 'in time'. John further relates the Word to creation. The existence of the world is the result of His creative activity. Through Him were all things made. He came into the world as the light which lighteth every man. But He came in a personal form as the Word made flesh. In this world of His own making He showed Himself as imminent light and incarnate person. The word is finally related to personal experience. He came to His own world but those who were His own people did not receive Him. But to as many as receive Him to them He gives the rightful authority to be called children of God.

John is, therefore, saying no small thing in his reference to Christ as the Word. He is, in fact, making use of a term which expressed the absolute nature of Christ as Divine. In Him as the Word made flesh, the eternal self-revealing God was incarnate.

Further reading:
C. J. Wright, *Jesus the Revelation of God*, 64 f. (London, 1950).

CHRIST AND LORD

With the exception of His birth name 'Jesus', no other has rooted itself so firmly in the thought of the world as that of 'Christ'. This name is the Greek equivalent for the Hebrew 'Messiah', which is rendered into English as the 'Anointed'. Originally it was a title, but soon it became a Name, the article being dropped. It came to be combined with the name Jesus either in the form 'Jesus Christ' or 'Christ Jesus'; and both Matthew and Mark announce that they are presenting the record of 'Jesus Christ'.

On a number of occasions Jesus refers to Himself as the Christ. Matthew has some nine references, Mark five and Luke nine. On twenty-four occasions others refer to Him as the Christ in the Synoptics—some of these are, of course, parallel accounts. In John's Gospel, too, the name appears frequently, but here its title aspect is several times stressed (e.g. 1. 41). In this verse the identity of Jesus with the expected Messiah is made clear.

In the Old Testament the king was referred to as the Lord's 'anointed' (Ps. 18. 50) in virtue of the pouring upon him of the sacred oil which was a symbol of the Spirit of God. Out of the failure of the kings, reinforced by the prophetic word, grew the expectation of the coming ideal King who would fulfil the hopes of Israel. It is this Ideal Figure who is pictured in Isaiah 11. 1-5. In the Second Psalm the title 'Messiah' (Anointed) is attached to this expected One, and as more and more the hope of the appearance of the Coming Deliverer grew in Israel the more the simple title 'The Messiah' was referred to Him. So it was that in the hey-day of the Baptist's ministry 'all men mused in their hearts concerning John, whether he were the Christ' (Luke 3. 15). It need cause no surprise that Jesus should rebuke the devils for proclaiming abroad the fact that He was the Christ. This was possibly because of the Jewish colourful notion of their coming King as a warrior with pomp and power; and for the further reason that He would have the discovery made at first-hand by those who would follow Him. At the same time there were vital moments in His life when Jesus declared His identity with the expected Messiah.

There was the occasion in the synagogue of Nazareth (Luke 4. 18, 19) when He took to Himself the prophetic words of Isaiah 61. 1-2. The word 'anointed' in the passage He read as being fulfilled in Him must have suggested the 'Anointed One'. This particular Scripture is significant since it reveals a Messiah not after the national pattern of the Jewish dreams, but a 'Servant of the Lord' whose mission was to bring spiritual enlightenment and salvation to the poor. In Matthew 11. 3 the question of the Baptist can hardly leave us in any doubt who was the personage intended or what was the force of our Lord's reply. In the crisis of Caesarea Philippi (Matt. 16. 16) Jesus drew from His disciples the acknowledgement that He was the Christ and He manifestly rejoiced in their testimony. He had secured the confession of His messiahship, now those disciples were to learn what manner of Messiah He was. (cf. Matt. 16. 21). Then at the trial He was asked the direct question about the reality of His messianic claims. And being put on solemn oath by the priests He declared that He was (Matt. 26. 63f). Jesus was crucified because He confessed His messiahship. The passage Matthew 26. 63f is important as uniting the three titles, Messiah, Son of Man and Son of the Blessed. For the believers of the primitive Church, then, the Jesus whom they revered and worshipped was very Christ, the Messiah of God.

In the Old Testament, however, not only was the King anointed; so, too, was the priest. In fact, in some passages the High Priest, as distinguished from the ordinary priests, appears to wear the semi-title 'the Anointed Priest' (cf. Lev. 4. 3, 5, 16; 6. 22, see Exod. 28. 41; 30. 30 etc.). Thus is Christ the Messiah, the regal Priest and the priestly King. As we move on into the rest of the New Testament we find that 'Christos' is now a proper name since its messianic significance expressed in the title 'The Messiah', 'The Christ', is less meaningful to the growing Gentile churches. But the essential facts of His kingship and priesthood remain, and the name itself becomes associated with others such as 'Son of God' and 'Lord'. In such associations it becomes 'charged with deep religious meaning'. It would seem, indeed, that what was regarded as important about Christ was not the office He held but the person He was. It was this which gave meaning to His work for us. He is, therefore, as Paul says using the fullest title for Him, 'our Lord Jesus Christ'.

Like the term Christ, that of Lord can be seen to

become more and more charged with deep religious meaning. The Greek word Kurios, either with or without the article, occurs over 240 times in the Gospels. This large number of instances is, however, obscured by the fact that many English words are used as equivalents; for example, it is sometimes translated 'master' (Matt. 15. 27), sometimes 'Sir' (Matt. 21. 30), sometimes 'owner' (Luke 19. 33). The fundamental significance of the term is that it describes one who has power or authority over persons or things. It implies ownership, and as such is used as a title of courtesy or reverence. In many places it is addressed to Jesus in this way or is used as a name for Him. It is found in the speech of His disciples without the article (cf. Matt. 14. 28), 'Lord if it be thou bid me come . . .' It is, as is to be expected, more frequent in the Fourth Gospel, since it records in fuller detail the private intercourse between Jesus and His disciples. Jesus also applied it to Himself (Matt. 7. 21); and it is referred to Him by the Shepherds (Matt. 2. 11). Without the article, then, the word appears as a name. But it also occurs in many instances with the article as a title. In this sense Christ applies it to Himself (Jn. 13. 13). The historical application of the title is found most frequently in Luke (18 times) and John (12 times). Most of John's instances are found in the last two chapters and in passages which are peculiar to it. They deal with the risen life and were written at a time when the higher conception of His personality gave a deeper significance to the title, and when its confessional meaning was fully known. The adoring cry of Thomas (20. 28) is an illustration of how among Jewish Christians, a title of respect addressed to a teacher becomes one of divine honour. Within the Gospels themselves it becomes more and more clear that for the disciples the respect which was due to a teacher becomes a realization that He was more (cf. John 7.

21; Luke 5. 8). To the Jewish Christian Jesus was Messiah; to the Hellenistic Christian Jew He was 'The Christ'; to the Gentile Christian He was 'The Lord'. And all three are combined in the familiar name 'The Lord Jesus Christ'. The Christ is the Lord, the possessor and ruler of the kingdom of God.

In the rest of the New Testament the title Lord is frequent being found some forty-six times in the epistles. Throughout, the idea of sovereignty is maintained (cf. 2 Cor. 10. 8; 1 Thess. 5. 16; 1 Cor. 5. 2; 1 Thess. 4. 6; Rom. 14. 9; 10. 12; Phil. 2. 11). Thus we note that the title Lord which seems to have been general as a title of respect, bursting this limit to take on in reference to Jesus a recognition of a special relationship, thereby becoming a confession of His superhuman nature which is tantamount to an avowal of His Deity.

Further reading:
J. Knox, *Jesus, Lord and Christ* (New York, 1958).
V. Taylor, *The Names of Jesus* (London, 1959).
D. Cullmann, *The Christology of the New Testament* (London, 1959).
B. B. Warfield, *The Lord of Glory* (London, 1907).
L. Morris, *The Lord from Heaven* (London, 1958).
E. G. Jay, *Son of Man, Son of God* (London, 1965).

THE REDEEMING REALITY

How sayest Thou then that the Son of Man
must be lifted up?

Chapter Six

SOMETHING ON THE NATURE
OF HIS WORK

Frequently have Christians expressed their gratitude to God the Father for giving His Son, but far too seldom do we express gratitude to the Son for giving us the Father. From one essential point of view this is precisely what Christ has done. 'No one cometh unto the Father save through Me'. In the Son we encounter the Father (cf. John 8. 19; 14. 8 etc.). There is no other possibility of meeting God as Father except in Him who is declared to be Son of God. It is in His Sonship men become sons of God; in relationship with Him we can speak confidently of God in terms of 'Abba, Father' (Rom. 8. 15; Gal. 4. 6). In and through His unbroken Sonship man's broken sonship is restored.

Christ is not, however, a pattern of man's noblest endeavours. He did not come to stimulate our struggling God-consciousness; He came to deal with our deeper sin-consciousness. His purpose in the world is not to inspire men at their best but to redeem men at their worst. And to do that He must take account of man's sin, the real barrier in the way of man's approach to God. It is the very heart of the gospel that in and through Christ the way is opened up for man to re-establish his relationship with God, broken as a result of his sinful rebellion. What man supremely needs, therefore, is to hear the good news about God; the declaration that in Christ God has taken action on their behalf.

All this puts Christ in a special position. It makes Him the Mediator, not the medium of the holy grace of God. He is the Revealer, and in no way the rival of God. He is the Redeemer, and not just the champion, or even the example, of mankind. As Son of God He has brought and bought salvation, as only One who is such could do, or would. He is the divine forgiveness incarnate and made actual and available for man. He comes as One actually redeeming, and not merely as offering redemption; as the divine destroyer of sin's guilt; as the Eternal Salvation of God made personally vivid and historically visible. Jesus did not come to give us a gospel, He came to be the gospel. The good news is that a Saviour has come, born to die: born to raise the sons of earth, born to give them second birth. This makes Jesus different. Such work puts Him in a category apart. He is not simply the greatest of the prophets, not the noblest of spiritual heroes, not the profoundest of humanity's seers or the most exquisite of its saints.

The truth is rather that Calvary is the very throne of God and the Christ who suffered there was no martyr. 'As God was incarnate in Jesus, so we may say that the divine Atonement was incarnate in the passion of Jesus' (D. M. Baillie).

There is much that we would wish to say here, but we must content ourselves with emphasising two relevant statements.

THE UNITY OF CHRIST'S PERSON AND WORK

'The coming of the Son of God is His work' says Brunner. His very presence in the world is none other than the redeeming revelation of God. It is quite arbitrary to keep the subject of Christ's person separate from His work. False views can easily arise if the subordination is made either way—if His person is subordinated to His work or His work to His person.

When once the work is made supreme at the expense of His person a mere subjective or valuation view of Christ's person may result. This is the error in the Christology of such teachers as Schleiermacher and Ritschl. For the first of these Christ is virtually regarded as the sum of one's pious religious feelings. Schleiermacher views Christ as the archetype of the religious man. He differs from us by the measure of His native God-consciousness. His work is to stimulate our dormant God-consciousness rather than to save us from our awakening sin-consciousness. Ritschl conceives the 'Godhead' of Jesus to be little more than the expression of the worth that Christ has for the religious thought of the believer. He robs our Lord's Deity of any objective factuality. Christ is the Pioneer of man's appreciation of God and no more. His position is merely that of the historical position of privilege. The 'Deity' of Christ is only another way of saying that Jesus is superior to all men as the Founder of a spiritual and ethical kingdom.

On the other hand, if the work is subordinated to the person, the result could be equally disastrous and unbiblical. In this case faith could be altogether speculative. The person of Christ is here discussed apart from His saving work. Following this line some have reduced Him to a mere teacher of ethical precepts at one extreme. At the other extreme, some have ended up by paying Christ 'metaphysical compliments', to borrow a phrase from W. N. Whitehead; but without any heart experience of the work He accomplished.

The right balance is, however, to keep together the work and the person of Christ, as one indissoluble unity. The constellation of events which centres in the action of Christ and in His person is the subject-matter of Christianity. Throughout the ages this actuality of

Christ, who He is and what He has done and does, has been understood as the revealed truth, proclaimed as the essential gospel experiences as a redeeming reality and sung about with grateful wonder. It was the custom of the early Church Fathers to underscore the word 'is' and 'am' in such declarations as, 'He *is* the Word', 'I *am* the Door', 'I *am* the good Shepherd'. In this way they sought to emphasise the unity of the person and the work of Christ. The One who is the Door by whom we enter in to find salvation, and the One who as Shepherd gave His life for the sheep, is the 'I am'. Characteristic of Christian faith and experience is this fact of the unity of Christ's person and work.

Here is one example from a report written at the time of the Welsh revival in 1904: 'The whole revival is marvellously characterised by a confession of Jesus Christ, giving testimony to His power to save, His goodness and His beneficence, and the testimony merging repeatedly into outbursts of singing'. This is the authentic biblical note—the confession of Jesus Christ and testimony to His power to save. It is precisely by being Himself that Jesus has done for man what no other man could do and made divinely available to every man that which all men need.

Further reading:
Athanasius, *On the Incarnation* (several good translations available).
E. Brunner, *The Mediator*, ch. xv (London, 1934).
B. B. Warfield, *The Person and Work of Christ* (Philadelphia, 1950).
V. Taylor, *Jesus and His Sacrifice* (London, 1957).

THE UNIQUENESS OF THE WORK OF THE PERSON
His name shall be called Jesus for He shall save His people from their sins (Matt. 1. 21). Christ's own understanding of Himself was that as Son of Man He had come to seek and to save that which is lost (Luke

19. 10). It is one of the 'Faithful Sayings' of gospel faith that Christ Jesus came into the world to save sinners (1 Tim. 1. 15). 'To save', then, describes the mission of Jesus in the world. Yet, as we shall see when we discuss the title Saviour below, the name 'Saviour' occurs but once in the Synoptic Gospels. But the title once given implies what He was and is in His very nature (cf. Luke 2. 11; cf. 1. 47). He impressed His contemporaries with this as the purpose of His presence among them. The idea was in fact virtually forced upon those who had themselves no experience of His saving activity. 'He saved others', was the sneer at the Cross; but the very sneer itself makes evident that the conception of Christ as Saviour was widespread. There are five places in Luke's Gospel where the word 'salvation' comes (1. 69, 77; 2. 30; 3. 6; 19. 6), and in each case it refers directly to Christ. In some passages it is almost personified to become a virtual title for Jesus. The godly Simeon, who waited for the consolation to Israel, had it revealed to him by the Holy Spirit that the Child brought into the Temple was 'the Lord's Christ' (Luke 2. 25, 26). Taking Him in his arms he thanked God that his eyes had seen God's Salvation (verse 30; cf. 3. 6). In accepting the invitation of Zacchaeus, Jesus declared that in coming to him, Salvation had entered his house (Luke 19. 9).

In the Book of Acts the term salvation appears six times. As we should expect, in view of the purpose of the epistles as instruction of believers in the facts and implications of their experience of grace, the concept becomes frequent, being found thirty-two times; thirty-five if Revelation is included.

In view of the fact that the idea of 'saving' occurs most often in connection with Christ's healing miracles, the curative connotation of the term would be uppermost in the popular mind (cf. Matt. 9. 22; (Mark 5. 34; Luke

8. 48): Matt. 27. 42; (Mark 15. 31; Luke 23. 35): Mark 3. 4; (Luke 6. 9): Mark 5. 23; 6. 56; 10. 52; Luke 7. 50; 8. 36, 50; 17. 19; 18. 42). In Jewish thinking coloured by the Old Testament understanding, 'saving' was synonymous with healing.

But there are passages where the curative idea does not fit (see, for example, Matt. 8. 25; 14. 30; 24. 22; 27. 49). In other places a more 'spiritual' connotation of the term is required (cf. for example Mark 8. 35; (Luke 9. 24, note Matt. 16. 25); Matt. 10. 22; 24. 13; Mark 13. 13).

An important passage marking for us the fuller meaning of Christ's saving mission comes in the story of the Rich Young Ruler (Matt. 19. 23f). Here it is shown that 'to be saved' (verse 25), 'to enter into the kingdom of God' (24) and 'to inherit eternal life' (29), are three ways of saying the same thing.

The higher idea that stands in the background is, according to Vos, that of the transference out of the sphere of death into life. More particularly Christ's saving work is seen to be a spiritual deliverance of men from sin and the impartation of new life, fitting them for the kingdom of God which has begun now as the rule of God in their hearts.

Such is the Salvation of God as God's saving act in Christ. Central, however, to the whole idea of salvation is that of forgiveness (Eph. 1. 7; cf. 4. 32; see Acts 5. 31; 13. 38; 26. 18 etc.). The really new thing in the gospel is this: that Christ did not, as the teachers of old, declare forgiveness as a general truth (cf. Ps. 86. 5), He granted it as a fact in His own name and right. No prophet of Israel's past ever dared to take this honour to himself. Jesus embodied in Himself the forgiveness of God. The incident of the paralytic man (Matt. 9. 2-8; Mark 2. 1-12; Luke 5. 17-26) evidently made a deep impression in this respect, since it is recorded that the people wondered, praised God and acknowledged that a power properly and only of God had been demonstrated as being in the possession of this man, Jesus (cf. Luke 7. 36f).

But if the forgiving act of Christ is the centre of the salvation of God, then the astonishing act of Christ is the basis of it. The clear biblical fact is that when there is no atonement there is no gospel. The simplest of all gospel truths, which is also the profoundest of all theological enquiries, is that He bore our sins. Scripture, observes James Denney, converges upon the doctrine of the atonement. Here is to be found its dynamic centre which makes it a gospel for humanity. The assertion that God is love has no meaning apart from the work of Christ; God so loved the world that He gave His only begotten Son. To talk even of the love of Christ in separation from His Cross is to speak vaguely. He loved me and *gave Himself* for me is the biblical way of declaring Christ's love. Only in the Cross have both the love of God and the love of Christ demonstration, reality and saving significance.

But as the new thing in Christ's teaching was the assertion of the right, and the proof of the fact, that He could forgive sins, the decisive thing in His atoning work is its relation to forgiveness. 'To preach the love of God out of relation to the death of Christ, but without being able to relate it to sin—or to preach the forgiveness of sins as the free gift of God's love, while the death of Christ has no special significance assigned to it—is not, if the New Testament is the rule and standard of Christianity, to preach the gospel at all.'

It is only a Cross-centred gospel which takes seriously man's sin and need. It is through faith in the Christ who has wrought for us a good work that man is reconciled. At the Cross he is justified from all things. 'Redemption without atonement,' as Brunner emphatically declares, 'is in the last resort the conception of sin as something natural, like disease. Forgiveness without atonement means sin is conceived as error.' It is in the Christ of the Cross that God speaks His word of pardon and declares our acceptance in His Son.

There are some who would have us believe that it is the teaching of Jesus which is of saving value. Adherence to His words is the way of salvation. He certainly declared that His words are spirit and life (John 6. 63). But He clearly did not intend to divorce His words from Himself. His words have their life in His life and spirit in His Spirit. They have their value only because they are *His* words. They find their authority in Him. We cannot separate what He said from Who He is. Ultimately to receive His words is to receive Him; and to receive Him with His words is to receive what is our sorest need, His word of forgiveness through His Cross. He came to bring men to the kingdom of God, that through Him they might have eternal life as men forgiven. But He must needs suffer and die. He must be 'lifted up' on Golgotha's gibbet. His suffering and dying have, therefore, according to His own thought and word, some vital connection with this purpose of His coming.

Without doubt the cross was latent in Christ's filial and messianic consciousness from the first. But it was after the Great Confession at Caesarea Philippi that He proclaimed it. All three Synoptics introduce our Lord's express teaching concerning His death at this point (Matt 16. 21; Mark 8. 31; Luke 9. 22). His audience was now, not so much the crowds, as the Twelve; His method was not so much preaching, as teaching; His subject was not so much the Kingdom, as Himself and in particular His death. He makes it clear that the way of the cross is the way appointed for the Lord's anointed, if He is to accomplish His work. He must die, not by any outward constraint; not because the wheel of history He has taken in His hands is too much for Him. Rather is it because of an inward necessity in the fulfilment of His divine mission. He has come to seek and to save that which is lost; and to do this He must be taken and by wicked hands be crucified and slain.

Between His death and His saving work there is, then, a vital connection: it is in this way man may come to the kingdom as forgiven. His life given will be a 'ransom for many' (Matt. 20. 28; Mark 10. 45). It is by His surrendered life that the forfeited lives of men are liberated. And the blood of His cross will establish a new covenant (Mark 14. 22-24). His is sacrificial blood with propitiatory power. In His death there is salvation for man; such is Christ's own understanding of His work (cf. John 3. 16; 6. 51-53; 10. 11, 28; 12. 27; 15. 13; 17. 19). As Son, Christ came to do the will of the Father; and obedience to that will, for the sake of man's salvation, brought Him to the cross. Whatever man owes as a pardoned sinner to the love and mercy of God he owes to the death of Christ.

Of course, it will be inevitable that a fuller statement of the meaning of the cross could only come after the crowning event itself had taken place. It is no wonder, therefore, that the cross looms large in the inspired interpretation of Christ's person and work. For Paul and the rest, the doctrine of Christ's death was not a theology, but the gospel. And it is interpreted in a variety of ways, but always in the last in relation to man's full salvation. It is related to the divine love (cf. Rom. 5. 7f; 2 Cor. 5. 14; Eph. 5. 25) and to law (cf. Gal. 3. 13) and to man's sin (cf. 1 Cor. 15. 3; Gal. 1. 4; Eph. 1. 7; Col. 1. 14; Heb. 9. 28; 1 Pet. 3. 18). It is viewed as substitution (Rom. 4. 25; Gal. 1. 4; 1 Thess. 5. 10 etc.), as redemption (Gal. 3. 14; 4. 4; Eph. 1. 7; Col. 1. 13 etc.), as propitiation (Rom. 3. 24-26 etc.), and as reconciliation (Rom. 5. 10, 11 etc.).

Metaphor after metaphor is used to give some understanding of what Christ wrought in the cross. The feeling comes to us that there is more in the cross than can ever be put into words. So great is our salvation that the dictum is seen to be true: non uno itinere potest prevenire ad tam grande secretum—'not by one way only can we reach so great a secret'.

The red thread of salvation through the Blood of Christ the Son of God is woven into all allusions to the saving work of His person. It is the greatness, the glory and the grace of the divine Christ which everywhere shines forth. It is He and He alone who could, and He and He alone who did this great thing for us. It is at the cross He is understood. How sayest thou that the Son of Man must be lifted up? Why the cross? The cross will assure us of His greatness: When ye have lifted up the Son of Man from the earth then shall ye know that I am He? (John 8. 28). The cross will persuade us of His glory: I if I be lifted up from the earth will draw all men unto Me (John 12. 32). The cross will be the measure for us of His grace: 'As Moses lifted up the serpent in the wilderness, even so must the Son of Man be lifted up . . .' (John 3. 14). His cross is assurance, is attraction and is atonement.

The saving work of God is, then, the atoning work of Christ; and the reconciling work of the Father is the saving work of the Son. By His cross and passion, in gracious fulfilment of the loving purpose of the Father, Jesus Christ the Son of God has once and for all, on behalf of and instead of sinful men, made a full and a perfect atonement for the sins of the world, whereby the broken relation of man to God should be restored and the barrier to communion with God removed.

Such a study of what God has done in Christ and what Christ has done for us before God can only make the forgiven man want to add his voice to those who with

glad song ascribe: 'Salvation unto our God which sitteth
on the throne, and unto the Lamb' (Rev. 7. 10).

Further reading:
James Denney, *The Death of Christ* (London, 1905).
E. F. Kevan, *Salvation* (Grand Rapids, 1963).

Chapter Seven

SOME OF THE NAMES OF THE WORKER

THE LAMB OF GOD

It is to the 'record of John', the witness in the wilderness, that we owe the great declaration concerning Christ that He is the Lamb of God which taketh away the sins of the world. A very good case could be made out for the thesis that in this John, son of Zacharias, we have the first and most impressive teacher of theology; the one who has given us the first and most impressive conception of Jesus Christ. John was certainly the first to identify the One who came to him to be baptised as gathering up in Himself all the strands of ancient prophecy and ritual relating to the lamb in the religion of Israel. In contrast with the successive statements and sacrifices of the Old Testament, in which a lamb of the flock has a central place, He is the lamb *of God*. As such He takes away the sin of the world. His is the act of God which He is. The Lamb of God—there is a whole theology in the title.

Discussion continues whether the background of the Baptist's declaration is the Pascal Lamb of Exodus 12. 3f, or the sacrificial Lamb of Isaiah 53. 7. In favour of the first is the fact that Jewish festivals appear to have had a special interest for the writer of the Gospel. Against the identity, however, point is made of the fact that the Pascal Lamb had no specific reference to sin. It should be noted, on the other hand, that the blood of the lamb in Exodus was the sign and the seal of salvation (cf. Exod. 12; 1 Cor. 5. 7; 1 Pet. 1. 18, 19). The second suggestion has special appeal by reason of the fact that in the passage in Isaiah the word 'amnos' is used in the Septuagint and is the same as occurs in John the Baptist's declaration. John, as did the eunuch on a later occasion, seems to have been meditating particularly on the prophecy of Isaiah, since he quotes from chapter 40 the day before.

Others, noting the tenderness of the lamb to whom reference is made in Jeremiah 11. 19, 'I am like a gentle lamb that is lead to the slaughter', consider this to have been the source of the Baptist's affirmation concerning Jesus. The passage concerning the Jewish ritual of the lamb slain at the morning and evening sacrifice (Exod. 29. 38-46) is thought by some commentators to be the more likely background of the words of John.

Too much effort, it seems to us, has been expounded in seeking to link what John declares with a limited or specific Old Testament passage. The fact is rather that a lamb having relation to the sin, the need, and the worship of the people has a place of particular significance throughout the progressive revelation of God's saving intention in the Old Testament. It runs right through the whole unfolding record of the history of salvation. If Exodus tells us of the necessity of the lamb, then Leviticus may be said to specify the purity of the lamb—it must be a lamb without blemish. Isaiah suggests the personality of the lamb—*He* is brought as a lamb to the slaughter. But it was left to John the Baptist, the last of the prophet's, to affirm the identity of the Lamb.

Fundamental to the use of the term in the context of God's purpose of grace for mankind is the idea of sacrifice. For the Baptist the One who had come to him to be baptized with the baptism unto repentance was seen to be here identifying Himself with man's sin. The Lamb of God, it was disclosed to John, He must be—the Lamb upon whom the Lord was laying the sins of the world.

From the beginning, the Lamb of God is seen to be one and the same with the Messiah who was to come (cf. John 1. 29, 36, 41). The Messiah expected was a personage of high worth. Could it be that John's spiritual knowledge had gone deeper than we have hitherto supposed and that it was as a result of his not seeing the glory element to be obvious that he found himself giving away to passing doubt? (Matt. 11. 2f).

In the year that king Uzziah died the prophet of Israel saw the Lord high and lifted up, majestic and glorious. That was his first dazzling vision. Then as he waited and watched he saw again. This time he saw One as a Lamb brought to the slaughter. First looks are not always conclusive. We have to go deeper and to look longer if we are to get to the full truth. Isaiah saw the Lord and Isaiah saw the Lamb. Did he identify them for himself? We do not know. John the Baptist certainly did. He saw the Lamb as the Lord, and the Lord as the Lamb. He bid his followers to behold Him as the Lamb of God which taketh away the sin of the world. In one great act of faith he saw the excellency of the Lamb's person: He is the Lamb of God. And he saw the efficacy of the Lamb's sacrifice: which taketh away the sin of the world. By the use of the term, then, there is described the mission of Jesus, as One standing in a special relation to God, as including an expiatory sacrifice of Himself for the sins of the world. It gives point to and explains the *modus* of what is more generally declared by Christ as being significant of His own coming in such passages as John 12. 47, 'I came . . . to save the world'.

Taking the whole sacrificial system, culminating in the Passover, and finding its highest reaches in Isaiah 53, there is the Lamb in prophetic vision. In the Book of the Revelation the work of the Lamb is given an eternal context (5. 6; 13. 8). Here is stressed the reality of the Lamb's sacrifice and the royalty of the Lamb's throne.

The sacrificial significance of the title is either clear (Rev. 5. 12; 13. 8; cf. 5. 6, 9; 7. 14) or implied (Rev. 5. 8, 13; 6. 1, 16 etc.) whether the word used is 'amnos' as in John 1. 29, 36; Acts 8. 32; 1 Pet. 1. 19, or 'arnion' as in Revelation. At the same time it is made very clear that the One who accomplished this sacrificial work for men is One most intimately related to God. He is of such a nature that what He had done carries with it the impress of His timelessness (cf. Rev. 5. 6; 13. 8; Heb. 9. 12, 14; 13. 20). In the term Lamb, or the extended one of the Baptist's declaration, the Lamb of God, the work and the person of Christ are vividly and vitally related. Such is His sacrificial work that it can be understood only as that of One who is both human and divine.

THE ONE MEDIATOR

Although Christ is explicitly referred to as the Messiah on four occasions only, and even here three of the four instances have the same context (cf. Heb. 8. 6; 9. 15; 12. 24), the idea of His mediatorship is basic to the whole New Testament. So fundamental, indeed, is the mediatorial conception that in seeking to give effective account of what Christ is in Himself and what He does for man's salvation, Emil Brunner suggestively entitles his lengthy exposition, *The Mediator*. It is on the character of Mediator that the other characters of the Saviour depend; it is the root of which they are the different branches; the office of which others are but the several component parts.

It is in the title Mediator that the person and work of
Christ the more obviously coalesce. It is His reconciling
work of mediation which provides the proper evangelical
foundation for a doctrine of the Person of Christ. In
very truth the decisive importance of Christ is that He
is the One who can do this for us. As Mediator, Jesus
stands for God before man, and for man before God.
Christ's place in the world is not simply that He *was*
something, but, more specifically, that being what He
was, He did what He did. As Mediator Jesus confronts
us on God's behalf and in Him God acts decisively for
us. In Him God meets us since here in Him our sin
was dealt with in judgement and in mercy. His presence
and His work in the world, and for it, are God's greatest
gift to man.

He in whom God meets us is the One in whom man
can meet God. Through a life and a work truly human
does God come to impart life divine. Jesus Christ is the
'middle term' in which God and man come together:
in Him they find their context. For to effect a real
mediation, the Mediator must be Himself both human
and divine. If Jesus had been a shadowy figure only,
and not really man, He might somehow have conveyed
an illusion but He could not have been the Mediator;
and if He had been a titular god only, and not really God,
He might have been a martyr, but He could not have been
the Mediator. No inspiration however noble, and no
impartation however full, could have fitted Him to be
the Mediator. No one of the Old Testament prophets
and no one of the angelic host could have been the
Mediator in the highest biblical sense. The only One
who can meet the requirements is He who had of old
His place 'in the bosom of the Father' (John 1. 18),
and who 'became flesh and dwelt among us' (John 1. 14).

His mediatorship is not an office conveyed to Him by
grace nor a place accorded to Him as reward. 'He bears

the name Mediator because He *is* what it expresses.'
All other titles of Christ have their centre and their
significance here. It has been suggested that the title
Mediator is specifically soteriological; but is not the case
that the soteriological interest is present in every reference to Christ throughout the New Testament? In
ontological passages, passages, that is, which are held
to be particularly concerned with the nature and being
of Christ, it is their salvation purpose which gives to
them their importance in the eyes of the writers. Soteriological titles are, therefore, rich in ontological significance as are ontological ones weighed with soteriological
content.

The word Mediator, as such, does not occur in the
Authorised Version of the Old Testament, although the
Greek word (mesitēs), translated Mediator in the New
Testament, does occur in the Greek Old Testament,
where it is used to render the Hebrew word 'mokiach'.
In the passage, the AV has 'daysman' (Job 9. 33), and
the RSV and the RV margin have 'umpire' (cf. Job 16.
21). Job finds himself unsure in the presence of God.
He would that he had an 'arbiter'—someone who
could act as a 'go-between', and mediate between God
and him. The New Testament provides the answer to
the complaining sigh of Job. There is One who stands
between God and mankind: One who as Man sits on the
throne of God. In Him the race has its 'daysman' betwixt
itself and God—One Who can 'lay His hand on
both'.

Israel of old had a mediator in Moses through whom
the law was given (Gal. 3. 19; cf. John 1. 17), and who
'stood in ' for his people in the days of their sin and
peril (cf. Exod. 32. 11f etc.). From the days of Philo
the title Mediator was in general use as a designation of
Moses who had represented the people of Israel before
God in the crisis days of their history, and more

particularly as the one to whom God communicated His words of Covenant.

In two New Testament books the word Mediator is referred to Christ: in the Epistle to the Hebrews He is set forth in connection with the foundation of the new covenant; in I Timothy (2. 5), it is the reconciling activity of the Mediator which is stressed.

Christ is the Mediator of the New Covenant (Heb. 8. 6; 9. 15; 12. 24). At the institution of the Last Supper, Jesus referred to the Cup as the New Covenant in His Blood (Matt. 26. 28). In Exodus 24, Moses, the mediator of the law, read the words of the covenant and heard the people's promise of obedience, and then sprinkled both the book and the people (cf. Exod. 24. 6-8; Heb. 9. 18f). In this way he ratified the covenant between God and the congregation of Israel. In like manner has Christ become the Mediator of the New Covenant by ratifying it with His own blood shed for the remission of sins. Thus is Christ revealed by contrast, as the true Mediator of 'a better covenant established upon better promises' (Heb. 8. 6). His is 'a better testament' (7. 22) based upon a 'better sacrifice' (9. 23), by reason of the 'blood which speaketh better things than that of Abel's' (12. 24). Thus by a 'better hope' (7. 19) is assured to those who are 'purged' of their sin (9. 14f, 22), 'sanctified' (10. 29), and have 'access' by the blood of Jesus (10. 19), 'to a better possession' (10. 34) and 'a better country' (11. 14). For this reason is the Mediator of the New Covenant 'better than the angels' (1. 4).

In the passage in I Timothy, the apostle argues that God, who is the Saviour of all those who believe, wills also the salvation of all men (1 Tim. 2 1f.). The One who acts as Mediator is the One who is 'God our Saviour'. But He took our common nature and in that nature offered Himself for the salvation of mankind. This is the special point the apostle wishes to emphasise.

The One who has taken the place of Mediator has, from the human point of view, all the necessities to make His mediatorship humanly actual. The Mediator is real, full and perfect Man. While this is the stress which Paul here wishes to make, he implies clearly that if He were man and man only He could not identify Himself with humanity as He has done. He has come to us from beyond the gulf that divides man from God, from beyond the breach which separates and which no man could span. He belongs to us fully, yet He does not belong to us finally.

As Mediator of the New Covenant and as the One Mediator between God and man, Jesus has, then, at once the divine dignity and the human status which constitute Him the sole 'Daysman' between God and man. Christologically, therefore, the term Mediator is of utmost significance. It is the fundamental truth of the gospel that in Christ, man is united with God. He is the bond wherein the mediation is accomplished and realized. Out of this truth every other truth connected with our 'so great salvation' flows; and in this fact every other fact about 'Jesus Christ the Lord' converges. For essential to the Mediator are the twin realities of that Humanity through which He is ours, and that Deity by which He is God's. 'To be Mediator means that He stands alone.'

Closely allied with the idea of Mediatorship are those of Intercessor (Heb. 7. 24, 25; cf. Rom. 8. 33f), and Advocate (1 John 2. 1). As Mediator Jesus has gained 'access' for us into the presence of God. As Intercessor, He acts to further our petitions with the Father. As Advocate, He answers every charge that sin and the devil can lay against us and He represents our case and cause in such a way as, at all times, to clear the guilty.

THE SAVIOUR OF MEN

It was the Samaritans who believed unto eternal life

after Christ's personal appearance among them who, according to John's Gospel, gave to Him the high title of 'the Saviour of the world' (John 4. 42). It was the fact of His own presence as the transformer of human life, following on the testimony of the woman He had met by the well-side, which called out this profound confession. The Samaritans more readily than the Jews would have appreciated the wider significance of Christ's mission. 'It was necessary that He should pass through Samaria', says the Evangelist. But this necessity was not a matter of geography, but of grace. There was a direct route to Galilee but Jesus did not take it. He would pass the way of Samaria and thus come to a mongrel race hated with a bitter hatred by the Jews. 'With two nations', said the Son of Sirach, 'is my soul vexed, and the third is no nation: they that sit upon the mountain of Samaria, and the Philistines, and that foolish people that dwelleth in Sichem'. The Samaritans were cursed in the Temple and their food reckoned unclean as the flesh of swine. It was to such people that Christ came. By the sheer graciousness and glory of His own person He created that impression which was given statement in the faith of those who saw Him as One desired, as 'the Saviour of the World'.

The term Saviour (Sotēr), as that of Mediator, is significant of all that as divine Person He had come to do. He had Himself first, and after Him the writers of the New Testament, used the term 'to save' as a comprehensive one to describe His mission. The New Testament is punctuated with evidence of the saving action of Christ and with the proclamation of the fact. Faith in Christ as Saviour, in the event which took place 'once and for all' in the atoning work of the cross, is the Christian religion. In distinction from all other forms of religion, the Christian gospel proclaims itself as faith in Jesus Christ as 'our God and Saviour'. It is the assured revelation of the whole New Testament that there is no possibility of everlasting life except through faith in Him in whom God comes to man; in whom there is the self-movement of God in which revelation consists and salvation is known. Thus are the centre and the foundation of the entire Christian faith seen to be 'Christological'; it is faith in One in and through whom we have the salvation of God.

Prominent, however, as is the idea of salvation in the New Testament, the formal title 'Saviour' applied to Christ is by comparison infrequent. It does not occur at all in Matthew or Mark. In Luke it comes twice (1. 47; 2. 11). The first of these references is to the angels' announcement of Jesus as 'a Saviour, which is Christ the Lord'. Without going into any discussion of how these collated designations are to be construed, it seems that there were united in the angelic message two lines of prophetic hope. The One who was born was connected with the promised advent of Jehovah for the salvation of Israel and at the same time He was the One who fulfilled the predictions of the coming of the Davidic King. Such a One is the Saviour—He who is promised Messiah and sovereign Lord.

In the other Lucan writing, the Acts of the Apostles, there are just two passages where the term occurs (5. 31; 13. 23). He is a 'Prince and Saviour' in 5. 31 (cf. 3. 15; Heb. 2. 10). In 13. 23 He is declared to be the Saviour of Israel. And this Saviour, it is further maintained, is of the seed of David (verse 23), yet, in the same context He is stated to be the begotten Son of God (verse 33), and the Holy One who saw no corruption (verse 34f).

Apart from the later Pastoral letters the term comes twice only in Paul's other epistles (Phil. 3. 30; Eph. 5. 23), although in all the apostle's writings the saving grace of Christ's person and work is everywhere treated.

There is no reason, therefore, to accept Harnack's contention that these meagre references (he does not of course admit the Pastoral Epistles as genuine writings of Paul's) show a studied avoidance of the title on Paul's part.

In the Philippian letter, a 'captivity' epistle, Paul declares that 'our citizenship is in heaven ('We are a colony of heaven' Moffatt), from whence we wait for a Saviour, the Lord Jesus Christ'. The apostle is making the point that salvation in the complete reality of it involves the redemption of the body. It is for this we wait the Saviour whose power it is to subdue all things unto Himself. In Ephesians Paul deals with the subject of the mutual relationships between husband and wife which he considers to be a partial parable of that between Christ and His Church. He declares Christ to be 'the Saviour of the body', which is the Church He loved and for which He gave Himself (Eph. 5. 23, 25).

It is in the Pastorals, however, and in II Peter that the title Saviour becomes frequent. Paul introduces himself in I Timothy as 'an apostle of Jesus Christ, by the commandment of God our Saviour and the Lord Jesus Christ' (1. 1). Here the Saviour is specified as being God (cf. 2. 3; 4. 10; Tit. 1. 3; 3. 4). But no less definitely is the term given to Christ (cf. 2 Tim. 2. 10; Tit. 1. 4; 2. 13; 3. 6). This epithet used thus interchangeably of God and of Christ can mean only that in the apostle's mind there was the complete and ready assimulation of Christ with God. In this way a background is provided for the interpretation of the passage Titus 2. 13, which, in contrast with His first coming in grace, speaks of the impending appearance of, as it should we believe be read, 'our great God and Saviour Jesus Christ' (cf. 1 Tim. 6. 14-16; 2 Tim. 4. 1-8). The saving work of Him who is Saviour is given a place among the 'Faithful Sayings' (1 Tim. 1. 15). He gave Himself to redeem us

(Titus 2. 14), and by His grace we are justified (Titus 3. 7). In the day of His appearance this Jesus will be revealed for what He is, 'the blessed and only Potentate, the King of kings and Lord of lords' (1 Tim. 6. 15).

In II Peter the title Saviour is specially associated with some one or more other names for Christ, while the simple 'Jesus', and even the simple 'Christ', do not occur at all (2 Pet. 1. 1, 11; 2. 20; 3. 2, 18). Such a reference to Christ as Saviour becomes more significant when it is recalled that in several Old Testament passages Jehovah is specifically and exclusively declared to be the only Saviour of His people. There is none beside Him (cf. Isa. 43. 11; Hos. 13. 4; cf. 1 Sam. 10. 19; 14. 39; 2 Sam. 22. 3; Ps. 7. 10; 17. 7; 107. 21; Isa. 43. 3). Jehovah is the Holy One of Israel, thy Saviour (Isa. 45. 15, 21; 49. 26; 60. 16; 63. 8; Jer. 14. 8). To call Jesus Christ, the Saviour, with this Old Testament knowledge in mind, is to make a deliberate transference to Him of a divine appellation. It can hardly be doubted that when Peter wrote he had in the background of his thought the promise of God to send 'a Saviour and a Mighty One' (Isa. 19. 20), and that the One he designates as 'our Lord and Saviour Jesus Christ' (1. 11; 2. 20; 3. 18) and 'our God and Saviour Jesus Christ' (1. 1) was this One. And the day of the Lord is the day of His appearing.

The title Saviour, then, does not only say something of what He does, it also unveils something of what He is. The word is applied to Jesus as a Divine title. Dr. Edwyn Bevan has shown that in the definitely non-Christian religions the figure of the Saviour is missing and that Gnostic systems borrowed its 'Soter' idea from Christianity. In answer to the question, What new thing did Jesus bring? Irenaeus replied, He brought what was new in bringing Himself. In bringing Himself He brought the salvation of God.

THE EXALTED REALITY
Ought not Christ to have suffered and to have
entered into His glory?

Chapter Eight

JESUS CHRIST . . .
CROWNED WITH GLORY

THE ENTHRONED LORD

Having endured the cross in the fulfilment and the filling full of all prophecy, Jesus Christ has taken His place of sovereignty and honour at the right hand of the majesty on high. It was not possible that death could hold Him (Acts. 2. 24). He who has life in Himself (John 1. 4; 9. 5) and whose purpose of grace it is to give life to whomsoever He wills, to them that believe (John 3. 36; 5. 4 etc.), could not be Himself contained in a tomb. He shattered the sepulchre, to bring life and immortality to light through the gospel (2 Tim. 1. 10). He lives as Victor over man's last enemy, death (2 Cor. 15. 26, 54). It is the constant affirmation of the New Testament that Christ is risen (Luke 24. 34; John 21. 14; 1 Cor. 15. 13f).

The epitome of the gospel as preached by the early Church is found in 1 Corinthians 15. 3, 4. He who dies for our sins, the apostle puts it elsewhere, was raised for our justification (Rom. 4. 5; cf. 5. 18). Only a Christ triumphant over the grave can explain the facts of the situation as experience attests it and as history records it. The changed outlook, the renewed zeal, the burning conviction, the missionary success of the early disciples and the expansion and continuance of the Church cannot be accounted for except on the certainty that He who was dead is alive again. If the resurrection were a delusion, a misconception or a trick, then the truth, goodness and love which are its results would have no foundation, and life itself would be a mockery. This one fact is the most sure and the most secure: Jesus Christ rose again from the dead.

Not only, however, did the first Church preach the news of the risen Christ, no less assuredly did it assert the glory of the ascended Lord (cf. Acts. 1. 2, 9, 11; 2. 33f; 3. 21f; 55f; 9. 3; 22. 6; 26. 12; Rom. 8. 34; Eph. 1. 20; 4. 10; Phil. 2. 9; 1 Tim. 3. 6; Heb. 4. 14; 8. 1; 9. 12, 24; 10. 12; 12. 2; 1 Pet. 3. 14). They knew Him risen and they saw Him ascend (cf. Mark 16. 19; Luke 24. 50-53). God highly exalted Him with a name above every name. He had declared before the high priest and the Sanhedrin that He would be accorded a place at the right hand of power. Now He is there; the enthroned Lord.

It is usual and seemingly right to mark Psalm 110 as the immediate Old Testament source of the conception of the ascension and session of the risen Christ. Our Lord, according to all three Synoptic Gospels, claimed the opening words of the Psalm as carrying a messianic significance (cf. Matt. 22. 44; Mark 12. 36; Luke 20. 42). It is quoted with the same understanding by the apostle Peter (Acts. 2. 34; cf. 1 Pet. 3. 22) and Paul (1 Cor. 15. 25), and the writer of the Epistle to the Hebrews (5. 4; 6. 20; 7. 7; 10. 12f). The practical bearing of Christ's enthronement is given a large place in the New Testament epistles, and its soteriological significance is also emphasised (cf. Rom. 8. 33f). More particularly it may be stated in summary fashion that it declares our Lord's reinstatement in His heavenly glory; it marks the completeness of His propitiatory sacrifice; and it assures the permanency of His priestly ministry.

The ascension of Jesus follows, indeed, from all the facts of His career: it is the natural consequence of who He had shown Himself to be in the service He rendered to His Father and the work He did for men.

From the Christological point of view it puts Him who assumed flesh within the Godhead. He returned to where He was no stranger. While within the human sphere He was not out of touch with the realm of His pre-incarnate glory, during the days of His earthly sojourn He continued the exercise of His cosmic functions.

Returning, however, to where He was before—to His place on the throne of God—He returned as something more than He was before. He brought back to the Right Hand of the Majesty on High His glorified Manhood. 'Christ ascended into the heavens not where the Word of God had not been before, seeing that He was always in the heavens and remained in the Father, but where the Word made flesh had not sat before' (Ruffinus). As surely as Jesus rose in a real human body glorified, so certainly was He raised to heaven in the same body. Paul makes quite evident the fact that He still inhabits a body in glory (cf. Col. 2. 9; Phil. 3. 21). When he speaks of the Redeemer, Paul seldom regards Him in any other light than as One who assumed humanity, and in that humanity He is now glorified.

The New Testament never sets the Incarnation of Christ as an isolated fact. It is always brought into organic union with the total truth about Him. Not only, that is, does it regard Him as the Word of God incarnate, but as the One who has enthroned glorified human nature in union with His deity. In the ascension Jesus threw off the restrictions of space—He went from the here to the everywhere—and in the heavenly world human nature reigns in His sovereignty. In that nature, glorified in union with the glory of His divinity, is to be found the hope and the goal of redeemed humanity.

On the throne of God reigns Jesus as the glorified Lord. We are bidden to come boldly to that throne (Heb. 4. 16). There is a King upon that throne, therefore we have ability. Art thou a king then? they asked Him. A King He truly is; but not of this world. The King is the one 'who can'—the one who is able. 'God sitteth upon the throne of His glory' sings a Psalmist—He is 'King of all the earth'. And there, too, in reigning splendour is the enthroned Lord—there is ability for those who need such grace. There is a Man upon the throne, therefore we have sympathy. The Carpenter of Nazareth reigns in eternal triumph; but He reigns as Man, as our Friend and our Brother. There is a Priest upon the throne, therefore we have representation. The prophet Zechariah saw in his vision 'a priest upon the throne'. Here we have in the enthroned Saviour the great High Priest who represents us fully and faithfully before our Father in heaven. There is a Lamb upon the throne, therefore we have salvation.

THE ENDURING PRIEST

While the conception of Christ as High Priest has hints elsewhere in Scripture (cf. Rom. 8. 34), and the High Priestly Prayer of John 17, it gets its fullest statement in the Epistle to the Hebrews. Broadly it may be said that the book of the Revelation is largely the vision of Christ the King and the Epistle to the Hebrews is our guide to all things relating to Christ as Priest. The title 'the High Priest' is used ten times in the epistle (2. 17; 3. 1; 4. 14, 15; 5. 5, 10; 6. 20; 7. 26; 8. 1; 9. 11). He is also 'priest' (5. 6), and 'a great priest' (10. 21).

In comparison with the general conception of their coming Messiah as the Anointed King, Jewish messianic expectations had little place for the idea of a Christ-priest. It was, however, characteristic of Christianity, under the illumination thrown back upon the promise of its fulfilment, to gather neglected aspects of the rich suggestions of the Old Testament and note their embodiment in Christ. This is particularly true in the case of the Hebrew letter in which the old covenant and the new are related and contrasted. It is specially striking that the writer should find in Psalm 110,which declares the Messiah not only David's Son but also David's Lord, a reference to Christ's priesthood: 'Thou art a Priest for ever after the order of Melchizedek' (Ps. 110. 4; Heb. 5. 6). In the High Priesthood of Christ we have all that is of lasting worth in the old covenant. The believers to whom this 'word of exhortation' came were being told by their Jewish critics that in following the Nazarene they were loosing all the rich splendour of their ancient leviticalism. The writer reminds them that far from loosing all, they were really gaining all in and with 'this man', declared to be the Son of God. Since they 'have' Him as High Priest, they have all that which is 'better' and 'eternal' and 'which cannot be shaken'.

At chapter 4. 14, the writer starts his discussion of the Priesthood of Christ. He begins with a statement on the personality of the High Priest. Not every man could be a priest; no man taketh this honour to himself (5. 4). So Christ glorified (doxazō) not Himself to be made a High Priest (5. 5). To Aaron it was an honour (timē) to be such. He was authorized to act for God on behalf of men. But to Christ it was more than an honour, more than an external authority conferred on Him. It was part of the glory inseparable from His Sonship. His office springs from His personality; it is not, as was the case with Aaron, a prerogative superadded. His High Priesthood was not 'from man'; not of the will of the flesh, but of God.

Under the symbol of the historic figure of Melchizedek, the writer emphasises what is the distinctive thing about our great High Priest. It is His 'foreverness'. Abraham's encounter with Melchizedek was with one who was then a priest. Whence he came and whither he went he could not say. There is no record of his birth or death; he just stood forth as a priest. So Jesus is no priest by 'physical descent or by legal enactments'. He is a Priest who is, at the same time, Son of God; a Priest of whom it is said, 'Thy throne, O God, is for ever and ever'. He ever-liveth in the glory of His sympathy and the greatness of His vocation—a Priest for ever.

In one central passage the writer presents his work in relation to His person (9. 13-14). The high priest of old came with the blood of bulls and goats. But He 'offered Himself'. Not now does any death avail us; only this. Here is sacrifice at its fullest. The high priests of the ancient leviticalism were not without blemish; but He was without sin. Here is sacrifice at its holiest. What He presents is His own blood, a sacrifice of infinite cost. Here is sacrifice at its costliest. He offered Himself 'through eternal Spirit'. Many able commentators interpret this, not as referring to the Holy Spirit, but as stating the nature and spirit of His high priestly offering. Thus the term 'spirit' is taken to describe the being of the Son as to His nature, and 'eternal' as an attribute of that nature (cf. 7. 3). If this is the way the phrases are to be understood, then it shows us sacrifice at its highest.

The writer stresses what he sees to be the special function of high priest. He has to do with 'things pertaining to God'. In his view this is Christ's unique function as High Priest. And He deals with God on behalf of men's sins. The High Priest and the Blood went together. Because he knows that every high priest 'is taken from among men' (5. 1), and thus 'appointed for men', emphasis is given throughout the epistle, as we have seen, to the humanity of Jesus. In vital ways, however, was the Jewish high priest unlike our great High Priest. His priesthood, unlike theirs, is not mutable and transient. The high priests of the old economy were men 'having infirmities'; but He was without sin. Ours is a great High Priest who is passed into the heavens where He is throned Priest-King. In heaven He lives for us and there His very life is His prayer.

Although the name 'High Priest' is connected with the work of Christ, it is no less significant for an understanding of His person. The One so described is declared to be 'this man', and also above the angels, occupying the throne of God. He is human and divine. And as Vincent Taylor remarks, 'the ministry which He fulfils brings Him into closest relationship with men, it is exercised 'before the face of God', and so is a service no man can render'.

Further reading:
H. B. Swete, *The Ascended Christ* (London, 1916).
W. Milligan, *The Ascension of our Lord* (London, 1898).
W. P. Du Bose, *High Priest and Sacrifice* (London, 1908).

THE EXPECTED KING

The concept of the Kingdom found a large place in the teaching of Jesus. So central and comprehensive indeed is it that it is not possible to speak of it without introducing the whole content of the Gospel. The conception was with Jesus all through His ministry. He began His preaching with the announcement that it was near (cf. Matt. 4. 17; Mark 1. 15), and on the eve of His death He still spoke of it and anticipated reunion with His disciples there (Mark 14. 25).

The idea of the kingdom was familiar to the Jews and the term was evidently in common usage (cf. 1 Chron.

28. 5; Dan. 2. 44; 4. 3). But by Jesus the kingdom-concept was enriched. From the very beginning the kingdom was specially that 'of heaven', or 'of God'; and it would seem that Jesus let His emphasis fall here so that in His mind it was something larger, and more spiritual than the Jewish state. Thus, however the idea of Jesus concerning the kingdom was rooted in the Old Testament it was certainly not confined thereto. The more He raised it above the popular notions the more sharply it became contrasted with them. The word kingdom suggests organization, association, location. But the term 'basileia' connotes rather rule, dominion. The term may be taken as a collective equivalent for that of Son of Man, which combines, as we have observed, humility and suffering with apocalyptic triumph in the future. These two senses unite in the term 'Kingdom of God' or 'of Heaven'. It has a present and a future reference. It is in process of development now and yet is to be revealed triumphantly in the future. It is the rule of God now in men's hearts, but is yet to come in apocalyptic glory. Of course, in every aspect of the kingdom, Jesus is the King. He reigns in the present through grace in the living experience of those who have come into the kingdom. He shall reign in the future when He is revealed in power and great glory as King, when every knee shall bow to Him and every tongue shall confess Him as Lord to the glory of God the Father.

The two outstanding features of apocalyptic thought are that the kingdom lies in the future and that it will come suddenly by the actual appearance of God. Throughout the New Testament these two ideas are brought into relation to Christ the ascended Lord. He is King upon the throne. In every epistle of the New Testament there is some allusion to the coming of Christ to reign. In the Revelation we have a picture of the final victory of God when the redeemed of all ages sing the Song of the Lamb to Him whose works are great and marvellous, the Lord God, the Almighty whose ways are righteous and true and who is Himself the King of the Ages (15. 3). Certainly the conflicts depicted in the book have an historic reference; and every victory of God is itself a judgement of God.

The book depicts the judging act of God as a series and in its consummation. The judgement as a series of acts is given in what is undoubtedly the kernel of the apocalypse, which begins with the opening of the sealed book in chapter 6 and ends with the outpouring of the bowls in chapter 16. Before the writer approaches the unfolding of impending judgement he unveils the heavenly and eternal background in front of which coming events are to be transacted (cf. chapters 4, 5). The seer gets behind the web of nature and history, and lets us see the Hand which sets these and all phenomena in the fabric of human experience. And the Hand is the Hand of Christ. God has pledged Himself to make an end of evil, and that cannot be done without cataclastic happenings in the world that lieth in the wicked one. In and through this cataclasm Christ is manifested as King.

The cycle of judgements leads on to the 'last judgement'. Throughout Revelation there is unfolded in the most impressive way judgement in its continuous execution and in its indubitable future. In every drama of the judgements of God, first and last, one name stands supreme. He is the Word of God, The King of kings and the Lord of lords. Thus 'the kingdom of the world is become the kingdom of our Lord and His Christ; and He shall reign for ever and ever' (11. 15).

Further reading:
Herman Ridderbos, *The Coming of the Kingdom* (Philadelphia, 1962).
G. E. Ladd, *The Gospel of the Kingdom* (London, 1959).

No names for Christ are more expressive than those by which John the Seer couples Him with God. He is Alpha and Omega; the First and the Last; the Beginning and the End (cf. Rev. 1. 8, 17; 2. 8; 21. 6; 22. 13). Here we have the fulness of Christ. He is the fulness of wisdom and knowledge. He is the fulness of space, for in Him and through Him and unto Him are all things. He is the fulness of time, for He fills eternity—before Abraham was I am; He is the One Who was and is and is to come; the same yesterday, to-day and forever. Here, too, is the finality of Christ. There is nothing beyond Him—nothing before, nothing after, nothing more. He has no 'before' and no 'after'. In this 'title of eternity' we have a solemn affirmation of Christ's eternal deity.

Thus is He 'the Yea and the Amen' authenticating the promises of God (2 Cor. 1. 20). He is, too, the principle of the creation of God (Rev. 3. 14). Jesus Christ is Ultimate. There is none before Him, nought beyond Him and nothing without Him. Other than Jesus will not do; less than Jesus will not suit; more than Jesus is not possible. More than all in Him we find. Everything of God is to be found in Him and little of God is to be found apart from Him.

> This man so cured regards the Curer, then,
> As—God forgive me!—who but God Himself,
> Creator and Sustainer of the world,
> That came and dwelt on it awhile!...
> And must have so avouched Himself in fact...
> The very God! think, Ahib; dost thou think?
>
> *Browning*

> My Lord and my God ... Saviour Divine
> With Glory Crowned.

> 'Thou seemest human and divine,
>   The highest, holiest, manhood, Thou;
> Our wills are ours, we know not how;
>   Our wills are ours, to make them Thine!
>
> *Tennyson*

LIST OF BOOKS MENTIONED IN THE FOREGOING PAGES

(Those marked with an asterisk are specially commended)

*Alexander, J. P., *A Priest Forever* (London, 1937).

Andrews, E., *The Meaning of Christ for Paul* (New York 1949).

Argyle, A. W., *The Christ of the New Testament* (London, 1952).

*Athanasius, *The Incarnation* (Several good translations available).

*Borchert, Otto, *The Original Jesus* (London, 1933).

Brunner, E., *The Mediator* (London, 1934).

*Denney, James, *The Death of Christ* (London, 1905).

— , *Jesus and the Gospels* (London, 1908)

Downer, A. C., *The Mission and Ministration of the Holy Spirit* (Edinburgh, 1909).

Du Bose, W. P., *High Priest and Sacrifice* (London, 1908).

*Edersheim, A., *The Life and Times of Jesus the Messiah*, 2 vols. (London, 1886).

Forsyth, P. T., *The Person and Place of Jesus Christ* (London, 1909).

Gardener-Smith, P., *The Christ of the Gospels* (Cambridge, 1938).

Humpheries, Lewis A., *The Holy Spirit in Faith and Experience* (London, 1911).

Jay, E. G., *Son of Man, Son of God* (London, 1965).

Jeremias, J. *The Central Message of the New Testament* (London, 1965).

— , *Abba* (Göttingen, 1966).

*Kevan, E. F., *Salvation* (Grand Rapids, U.S.A., 1963).

Knight, H. J. C., *The Temptation of our Lord* (London, 1922).

Knox, J., *Jesus, Lord and Christ* (New York, 1958).

*Kuyper, A., *The Work of the Holy Spirit* (Grand Rapids, U.S.A., 1964).

Ladd, G. E., *The Gospel of The Kingdom* (London, 1959).

Lewis, C. S., *Mere Christianity* (London, 1952).

Milligan, W., *The Ascension of our Lord* (London, 1898).

Morris L., *The Lord from Heaven* (London, 1958).

*Orr, James, *The Virgin Birth of Jesus* (London, 1914).

*Ridderbos, Herman, *The Coming of the Kingdom* (Philadelphia, 1962)

Robinson, J. Armitage, *Note on 'Beloved' in St. Paul's Epistle to the Ephesians* (London, 1903).

Sidebottom, E. M., *The Christ of the Fourth Gospel* (London, 1961).

*Smeaton, George, *The Doctrine of the Holy Spirit* (London, 1961).

*Stewart, James S., *A Man in Christ* (London, 1938).

Swete, H. B., *The Ascended Christ* (London, 1916).

Taylor, V., *The Names of Jesus* (London, 1959).

— , *Jesus and His Sacrifice* (London, 1957).

Ullmann, C., *The Sinlessness of Jesus* (Edinburgh, 1901).

*Vos, Geerhardus, *The Self-disclosure of Jesus* (Grand Rapids, U.S.A., 1950).

Warfield, B. B., *The Lord of Glory* (London, 1907).

— , *The Person and Work of Christ* (Philadelphia, 1950).

Wright, C. J., *Jesus the Revelation of God* (London, 1950).

LIST OF BOOKS SUGGESTED FOR
ADVANCED STUDY

(Those marked with an asterisk are specially commended)

Adam, Karl, *The Son of God* (London, 1937).

Andrews, H. T., *The Christ of Apostolic Faith* (London, 1922).

Baillie, D. M., *God Was in Christ* (London, 1947).

*Boettner, L., *The Person of Christ* (Grand Rapids, U.S.A. 1943).

Bornkamm, Gunther, *Jesus of Nazareth* (E. T. London, 1960).

Bosc, Jean, *The Kingly Office of the Lord Jesus Christ* (E. T. London, 1959).

Boslooper, T., *The Virgin Birth* (London, 1962).

Cerfaux, L., *Christ in the Theology of Paul* (New York, 1959).

*Craig, Samuel G., *Jesus of Yesterday and Today* (Philadelphia, 1956).

Creed, T. M., *The Divinity of Jesus Christ* (Cambridge, 1938).

Cullman, O., *The Christology of the New Testament* (London, 1959).

Curtis, W. A., *Jesus the Teacher* (Oxford, 1943).

Davies, J. G., *He Ascended into Heaven* (London, 1958).

*Denney, James, *The Death of Christ* (London, 1905).

Dibelius, Martin, *Jesus* (London, 1963).

Duncan, G. S., *Jesus, Son of Man* (London, 1947).

Edwards, Douglas, *The Virgin Birth in History and Faith* (London, 1941).

Fuller, R. H., *The Foundations of New Testament Christology* (London, 1965).

*Henry, C. F. H. (editor), *Jesus of Nazareth: Saviour and Lord* (Grand Rapids, U.S.A., 1966).

Higgins, A. J. B., *Jesus and the Son of Man* (London, 1964).

Hodgson, Leonard, *And Was Made Flesh* (London, 1928).

Hooker, M. D., *Jesus and the Servant* (London, 1959).

*Jay, E. G., *Son of Man, Son of God* (London, 1965).

Johnson, H., *The Humanity of the Saviour* (London, 1962).

Kennedy, H. A. A., *The Theology of the Epistles* (London, 1919).

Künneth, W., *The Theology of the Resurrection* (London, 1965).

*Ladd, G. E., *Crucial Questions about the Kingdom of God* (Grand Rapids, U.S.A., 1952).

*—, *Jesus and the Kingdom* (London, 1964).

—, *The Gospel of the Kingdom* (London, 1959)

Loos, van Der, H., *The Miracles of Jesus* (Leiden, 1965).

Lynch, W. E., *Jesus and the Synoptic Gospels* (Milwaukee, 1967).

*Macken, J. Gresham, *The Virgin Birth of Christ* (London, 1930).

Mackintosh, H. R., *The Person of Christ* (Edinburgh, 1912).
Manson, W., *Jesus the Messiah* (London, 1943).
Manson, T. W., *The Servant-Messiah* (Cambridge, 1956).
Moffatt, James, *The Theology of the Gospels* (London, 1912).
Morgan, W., *The Religion and Theology of Paul* (Edinburgh, 1917).
*Morris Leon, *The Lord from Heaven* (London, 1958).
*Murray, John, *Redemption: Accomplished and Applied* (Grand Rapids, 1955).
*Orr, James, *The Resurrection of Jesus* (London, 1908).
Otto, R., *The Kingdom of God and the Son of Man* (London, 1938).
*Owen, John, *The Glory of Christ* (London, 1933).
*Pache, Réne, *The Return of Jesus Christ*, (Chicago, 1955).
Ramsey, A. M., *The Glory of God and the Transfiguration of Christ* (London, 1940).
— , *The Resurrection of Jesus Christ* (London, 1946).
Ramsey, W. M., *The Christ of the Earliest Christians* (Richmond, Virginia, 1959).
Rawlingson, A. E. J., *The New Testament Doctrine of Christ* (London, 1926).
— , *Christ in the Gospels* (London, 1944).
Scott, C.A., Anderson, *Christianity according to St. Paul* (Cambridge, 1927).
*Shepherd, J. W., *The Christ of the Gospels* (Grand Rapids, 1939).
Smith, David, *The Days of His Flesh* (London, 1906).
Speer, Rober E., *The Finality of Jesus Christ* (New York, 1933).
Stalker, James, *The Christology of Jesus* (London, 1899).
Stauffer, E., *New Testament Theology* (E. T. London, 1955).
Stevens, G. B., *New Testament Theology* (Edinburgh, 1899).
*Stewart, James S. *The Life and Teaching of Jesus Christ* (London, 1953).
Strong, E. L., *The Incarnation of God* (London, 1920).
*Tait, A. J., *The Heavenly Session of our Lord* (London, 1908).
Taylor, Vincent, *The Person of Christ in New Testament Teaching* (London, 1959).
— , *The Names of Jesus* (London, 1959).
— , *Jesus and His Sacrifice* (London, 1937).
*Tenney, Merrill C., *The Reality of the Resurrection* (New York, 1963).
Thorburn, T. J., *The Doctrine of the Virgin Birth* (London, 1908).
Turner, H. E. W., *Jesus, Master and Lord* (London, 1953).
*Warfield, B. B., *The Glory of Christ* (London, 1907).
*— , *The Person and Work of Christ* (Philadelphia, 1950).
Whiteley, D. E. H., *The Theology of St. Paul* (Oxford, 1964).